TRUMP, CORONAVIRUS, BIDEN:

HOW IT ALL HAPPENED

As seen through the eyes of an Englishman in
New York

Peter J. Rolls

Fulton Books
Meadville, PA

Published by Fulton Books 2022

ISBN 978-1-63860-933-9 (paperback)
ISBN 978-1-63860-934-6 (digital)

Printed in the United States of America

Dedicated to Orlin Todorov Todorov
18 January 1962–13 December 2020

January 2020

Begin at the Beginning

What follows is the view of an Englishman, me, living under a stay-at-home order in New York. It is a view of how the coronavirus pandemic in the US is being overseen by a certain Captain Clueless, an incompetent orange man who is totally out of his depth. Sadly, at the time of writing, this man is also president of the United States of America.

When It Began

A 2020 New Year's present to the world came from China on 31 December 2019 in the form of a brand-new and as yet unnamed virus. At this point, while health experts around the world were concerned, no one was yet ringing alarm bells.

The situation began to evolve quickly, and as early as 17 January, cases are confirmed by the World Health Organisation (WHO) in China, Thailand, Japan, and South Korea. France and Australia also reported their first cases.

On 20 January, the first case in the US is confirmed. The patient is a thirty-five-year-old man from Washington state who had returned from a trip to Wuhan, China.

On 24 January, Trump tweets how the US greatly appreciates China's efforts and transparency and thanks President Xi.

However, concerns around the world increase as numbers in the Far East climb and the virus spreads to more countries. President Trump is asked if he is worried this could become a pandemic. "No, we have it totally under control. It's going to be just fine." By 30 January, all was still "very well under control." And even better, a couple of days later, he is on Fox News, saying, "We've pretty much shut it down." It's amazing how soon into this mess he displays how stupid he is.

We can argue that Trump had little reason to be concerned at this early stage; but as president, he should at least have expressed a note of caution or concern, but not him. He thinks he's Captain Pickard on the *Starship Enterprise*. "Coronavirus? I want rid of it. Make it so, Number One!"

On 30 January, the WHO steps up its level of concern, declaring the virus a global health emergency, and Trump blocks travel from China, although the two actions are not linked. That same evening, the chump-in-chief holds a rally in Iowa, saying, "We think we're going to have a good ending for it." So Wanknuts has solved the problem by banning flights from China.

February 2020

The Virus Is Named

It's 4 February, and China announces some twenty thousand confirmed cases. This figure is shocking and highlights just how contagious this new virus is. It has now spread to twenty-three countries, but case numbers outside China are currently "low" at 159, with 11 in the US.

Today is also the day when the cruise ship *Diamond Princess* is quarantined in Yokohama, Japan. Within two days, more than forty people are to test positive, including eight Americans.

One week later, on 11 February, the WHO gives the virus its name: COVID-19 (COronaVIrusDisease-2019). So here we are, six weeks into this, and things are getting serious, right? Wrong! A few days later, Trump is dismissive of the situation, saying there are only fifteen people in the US diagnosed with COVID-19 and that they are all getting better. Bullshit!

A Small Digression—Tax Cuts

At this point, I should mention what's been happening in the stock markets, more specifically, the Dow Jones. Trump loves watching share prices rise, and on 12 February 2020, the Dow reached an all-time high of 29,500-plus. According to him, the strong performance was all down to him.

Actually, in part, it was. He had introduced a massive programme of tax cuts in December 2017, which included significant benefits to the already-rich and to corporates. The idea was that corporates would invest this windfall in their businesses and their employees.

So what did happen to the money? Well, the corporates used it to buy back their own shares, and the rich got richer. The tax cuts certainly added impetus to the markets, but let's ignore the fact that the cost needlessly initially adds US $1.8 trillion (that's $1,800,000,000,000) to the budget deficit between 2018 and 2028.

We all know that one trillion is a big number, really big, but just how big is it? Well, if you are given $1 trillion today and that amount had been accumulating at the rate of $1 million each day, the first $1 million would have been paid 2,740 years ago! (For $1.8 trillion, you have to go back to 300 years before the pyramids in Giza were built.) No wonder share prices rose tremendously, *so tremendously!*

Anyway, the Dow continues to climb; and on 19 February 2020, for the umpteenth time, Trump tweeted "Highest stock market in history by far." He was right, but that is without doubt the last time he will be able to make such a claim.

The following day, the WHO reports 77,000 cases in twenty-seven countries. The Dow drops by more than five hundred points, and a week later, it is more than four thousand points down from its all-time high. Aaahhhhggg! Trump is silent.

On 26 February, California has its first case; and the worldwide infected total is now 82,000, with 2,247 deaths. But no worries because Trump says the US is "really prepared" and puts his idiot VP, Mike Pence, in charge of a White House task force. Pence? Seriously?

This sycophant is about as useful as a chocolate teapot, but we are safe because a month later, he will start working with Trump's son-in-law, Jared Kushner—a real superstar, whose credentials to do anything other than standing around looking stupid are nonexistent.

However, despite California, Trump remains confident (for *confident*, read arrogant) and says the few cases in the US would soon be "close to zero" and, the next day, says, "It will disappear—it's like a miracle." The only miracle is that he ever became president.

Two days later, 28 February, the total number of infected continues to climb with increases being reported across Europe, pushing numbers worldwide up to 84,600 with 2,923 deaths. Bear in mind, despite all that is going on around him—namely COVID-19 cases on the rise, death rates increasing, stock markets everywhere in free fall—what does Trump do?

He goes to a rally in South Carolina and, referring to accusations that the Russians interfered with the 2016 elections, says the Democrats failed with "Russia, Russia, Russia, they failed with the [first] impeachment hoax, and now this is their new hoax." The man is a total knob-head!

He talks about having only fifteen cases in "this massive country" and "because of the fact we went early [stopping flights from China], we could have had a lot more. Our country is doing great." WTF? He is still not with it! And he refuses to accept what is right under his button nose.

On top of this, that odious lowlife, Don, Son of Don says in an interview with Fox News, "For them [the Democrats] to try to take a pandemic and seemingly hope that it comes here and kills millions of people so that they could end Donald Trump's streak of winning is a new level of sickness." No, my friend, it is with you that a new level of sickness lies.

Biden Wins Carolina Democratic Primary

Joe Biden announced his candidacy in the 2020 presidential election back in April 2019. His progress through the primaries is not spectacular, but everything changes on 29 February when he wins a landslide victory in the Carolina primary. And this victory marks a key turning point for him. His competitors drop out and give their backing to Biden, and he quickly becomes the presumptive Democratic presidential nominee.

Biden's victory in Carolina was due entirely to Democratic congressman, Jim Clyburn, a longtime politician and today the

House majority whip. He put his full support behind Biden and, in doing so, brought with him the significant Black vote. As we will see, Biden later goes on to appoint Kamala Harris as his running mate.

This Is Not Going Away

On 29 February 2020, the US has its first death. Total cases worldwide are 88,400 with 75 in the US.

Things are now moving faster, and it's apparent that Trump's "close to zero" promise is in the wind, along with every other promise he makes. To allay concerns about numbers, Trump demonstrates just how away with the fairies he is and, on 3 March, announces, "We will have vaccines relatively soon."

What? According to all your medical experts, vaccines take twelve to eighteen months to become tried, tested, and available! He also adds, "We'll have not only vaccines but also therapies," and then helpfully explains, "Therapy is sort of another word for cure." Well thank you Mr. Thessaurus.

It's ironic that against all expectations, vaccines were indeed to become available by year-end. An incredible achievement, for which Trump does indeed deserve credit.

However, at his point, Trump is not giving the level of attention to COVID-19 that it warrants, but rather, his eye is on maintaining his base. None of his recent comments has any substance. He is giving no comfort, no advice, and no direction, despite calls from almost every quarter for him to do so. This becomes more evident as the situation unfolds.

In the meantime, the Dow continues on its downward path with an occasional good day thrown in for good measure and closes just shy of twenty-six thousand (on 3 March). Total COVID-19 cases are 93,016 (124 in the USA) with 3,202 deaths.

Things are now getting "stormy" but not the Daniels[1] type of stormy. El Pimpo is beginning to take some "incoming" because

---

[1]   Stormy Daniels is a pornographic film actress who had an alleged affair with Trump and was allegedly paid hush-money to keep quiet. Note to self: well

of the limited and late COVID testing and hospital equipment shortages, so the next day, he goes again on Fox News.

He is asked to respond to the criticism and does not disappoint. *It's Obama*—Obama and Sleepy Joe! "They didn't do anything about it [swine flu!]." What? Later that day in the White House, he continues to blame Obama. "The Obama administration made a decision on testing that turned out to be very detrimental to what we're doing." Yes, dear.

Confirmed coronavirus cases worldwide are still on the increase and are up to 95,300 with 3,285 dead.

---

done for saying "alleged"!

March 2020

COVID-19 Begins to Take a Real Hold

By 6 March, the worldwide number of cases tops 100,000, and it is today that Trump demonstrates yet again his total lack of leadership and complete unsuitability for his position. He boasts, "Our numbers are lower than just about anybody" (315 cases and fifteen dead) and blatantly lies by saying, "Anyone who wants a [COVID-19] test can have one."

The cruise ship *Grand Princess*, with over two thousand passengers, has just arrived in US waters and sits off the coast of California, waiting to dock. Can they dock? No chance! Captain Trump wants them to stay where they are.

Referring to the number of confirmed cases in the US, he says, "I like the numbers being where they are. I don't need to have the numbers double because of one ship." Bless him! In ten days' time, the number of infected in the US will rise to 4,600 with eighty-seven deaths.

On 10 March, Trump tells us, "[Things are] really working out. A lot of great things are going to happen."

What great things? We know he's talking crap because he always rolls out those meaningless wait-and-see lines when he lies, and indeed, no great things happen. In fact, quite the opposite.

To confirm his lack of any understanding of what is happening, he follows up the next day with "We are responding with great speed and professionalism." Well, that's a relief, especially as today the WHO officially declares COVID-19 a pandemic and Trump has done nothing to marshal resources needed to access the means to organise test kits! His comments again are aimed at his base.

Back to the Dow, which has again been jumping around. Trump has been silent on the matter recently, apart from the occasional predictable tweet following an up-day, such as his boasting of the one-day record rise of two thousand points on Friday, 13 March. Well done, sonny!

However, the trend has definitely not been his friend; and by Monday, the Dow is back down again, losing all of Friday's gains, closing at 20,200—more than 9,000 points off its all-time high a little more than one month earlier. But, hey, look on the bright side, at least you have another record!

Looking at some of his comments around this time, we can see the man is utterly clueless and has pretty much lost the plot, not that he had it in the first place.

12 March: "It's going to go away." He imposes a ban on travel from twenty-six European countries, adding the UK and Ireland a couple of days later. Needless to say, no one in Europe knew anything about it; and according to a BBC report, many European leaders were "incandescent with rage" at not being given any warning.

13 March: "I don't take any responsibility." What's new?

15 March: "It'll be great. We're going to be so good." Oh yes! Sooo good.

16 March: "It came up so suddenly." No, it didn't, you wanker. You were asleep at the wheel.

17 March: "THIS IS A PANDEMIC. I FELT IT WAS A PANDEMIC LONG BEFORE IT WAS CALLED A PANDEMIC. ALL YOU HAD TO DO WAS LOOK AT THE OTHER COUNTRIES." You absolute bloody plonker!

That's Not My Job!

We know that by March, hospitals are complaining of a shortage of protective gear. Governors of states with high case numbers are complaining that federal government is doing nothing to help with procurement.

True to form, Trump says it has nothing to do with him, but he's wrong. Normally, it would be for the Centers for Disease Control and Prevention (CDC) to coordinate distribution; but Trump had already slimmed it down in May 2018, shutting an office specifically dedicated to pandemic prevention, an office which had been established by—you guessed it—*Obama!*

In a *Washington Post* op-ed on 13 March, Beth Cameron, a former head of the pandemic office, said she was mystified why it was eliminated. "Our job was to be the smoke alarm—keeping watch to get ahead of emergencies, sounding a warning at the earliest sign of fire—all with the goal of avoiding a six-alarm blaze."

This lack of coordination leaves states scrambling for protective equipment, and they are forced to compete with one another. Governor Cuomo complains that the State of New York is paying more than $7.00 for a medical mask, instead of $0.70!

Testing is also a problem, and Trump again says the governors should sort these problems out for themselves, leaving his VP to talk crap on television. Pence appears on CNN and boasts that testing is going well; but when he is presented with figures posted on the CDC's website showing test numbers dropping, Pence is dismissive, saying they are outdated.

After a to-and-fro, Pence is then asked exactly how many tests have been done; and says, "Well I would leave that to the experts." *Whaaaat?* You're head of the task force, you idiot. You should be living and breathing these numbers!

However, from the beginning, the CDC has been found wanting—late testing, no testing, poor testing, poor test kits. They got off to a bad start, and many blame them for the lack of early testing and for the US being at the high level of infection it is.

Trump is in and out on this, but mostly out. When praise is given for good progress with testing, he puts his hand up in class and says, "Please, miss, that's me, miss. It's me. It's me." When there's criticism, he runs out of the classroom. He does not help the CDC by any of his actions.

Lockdown Time—"U Can't Touch This"

By mid-March, social distancing is reasonably well-established, but it's not working well enough. And the virus continues to spread. Social distancing alone is not enough, so most states put lockdown orders in place, meaning all nonessential workers are to stay home and everyone is to avoid outdoor group activities.

On 23 March 2020, Governor Andrew Cuomo puts the state of New York on lockdown—so no gyms, clubs, restaurants, pubs, or shops, excluding food stores and pharmacies. The impact on individuals, on all businesses large and small across the country is massive and immediate.

This experience, however, is being shared by communities and countries worldwide as each faces its own problems and adapts its own solutions. The number of cases in the US has now jumped to 43,781 with 555 deaths.

It is disappointing to note that while the majority of states in the US are in lockdown, not all have such an order in place. *The New York Times* reports that as of 2 April, "a small group of states—Arkansas, Iowa, Nebraska, North Dakota, and South Dakota—had no known lockdown orders in place. All of these states have Republican governors." Thanks to Trump, COVID-19 is becoming politicised.

Senate Approves $2 Trillion Rescue Package

In late March, in response to the pandemic, the Senate approves a massive $2 trillion rescue package. The good news is that whilst there was much discussion between Republicans and Democrats, the package gets full bipartisan support with 96–0 approval. Good to see.

Senate majority leader Mitch McConnell says, "From arguably the most partisan, divisive thing you could possibly do to coming together entirely, I think, says a lot about the United States Senate as an institution, our willingness to put aside our differences and to do something really significant for the country."

The plan is wide-ranging, giving cheques of $1,200 to people making up to $75,000 a year and $2,400 for couples making up to $150,000 with an additional $500 per child. Other provisions include $100 billion for hospitals, $350 billion for small businesses, $500 billion for corporations, and $150 billion for state and local stimulus funds.

April 2020

Coronavirus Numbers Up, Unemployment Claims Up

Over the last ten days or so, the rate of increase in cases both worldwide and in the US has been almost exponential; and by 2 April, the global case number breaks through the one-million mark, reaching 1,016,000 with 53,200 deaths. In the US, the numbers are 245,000 and 6,100, respectively, and rising.

We are now advised not to leave our homes at all if possible. These are horrible days.

Unemployment Claims—Up, Up, and Away!

Unemployment claims are seriously on the rise. In the week-ended 21 March, 3.3 million claims are filed. The following week, another 6.9 million claims; and as of 4 April, a further 6.6 million, bringing the total to 16.8 million, or around 11 percent of the labour force.

To put these numbers in perspective, the US Bureau of Labor Statistics produces data showing the weekly average of unemployment claims since 1970 is 350,000.

Today's numbers are terrifying, and Bank of America economists predict employers will cut between sixteen million and twenty million jobs, with the unemployment rate peaking at 15.6 percent between now and June.

Every day, we see and read about the lives of so many people whose worlds have been turned upside down and have no idea what the future holds for them. Their stories are heartbreaking and lead us to ask how and when we will recover from this nightmare.

Daily White House Briefings—240,000 Deaths Forecast for the US

10 April, today is a day of sad milestones, with worldwide deaths now reaching 102,684 and total cases in the US up to 502,876.

Trump recently began daily briefings from the White House pressroom. The purpose is to give a COVID-19 update to the nation and allow the medical professionals to share relevant news and information. However, instead of giving the floor to his medical team, he shamelessly uses these gatherings for self-promotion.

He announces that the White House coronavirus task force estimates deaths in the US could reach as many as 100,000 to 240,000. The range is so wide as to be meaningless, and no timeframe is given. But both Dr. Anthony Fauci, a leading member of the task force, and Trump say we are in for a bad two weeks as the death toll rises.

But Trump also provides us unwittingly with lighter moments, well, hilarious actually. The Reverend Don declares, "I'm a Christian."

What? No, you're not. Before you were elected, you couldn't even spell GOD. You're a hypocrite and an opportunist. You wanted the evangelicals, and you got them. Well done!

You've managed to expose the more extreme among them as being just as unprincipled and as ungodly as you are. You deserve one another—praise the Lord! If only you really did believe in heaven and hell, you could all go to that hot place together, where you belong.

Trump's "Meltdown Monday"—13 April 2020

Amazing! Today, Trump completely loses it. An article published over the weekend by *The New York Times* sends Dodgy Don spinning round the ceiling lights!

It points out that as far back as early January, he was warned of the potential for a pandemic; but "internal divisions, lack of planning, and his faith in his own instincts led to a halting response."

It also says that through January and February, coronavirus alarms were being sounded by government figures around him, but he wasted that time by doing nothing. So he's known for ages, but no matter, he never listens anyway.

El Lardo starts today's coronavirus briefing by assuring us he's done nothing wrong. He swipes at reporters and has a pop at Joe Biden. He says, "The story in *The New York Times* is a total fake. It's a fake newspaper, and they write fake stories." He then asks for the lights to be dimmed and introduces a video!

Are you kidding? The video is pure Trump propaganda, totally misrepresenting all his actions as being supported by everyone. And just like that, history is rewritten. "Hey, presto, Captain Perfect!"

Finally, after another dose of self-congratulatory bullshit, journalists get to ask questions, and now the fun really begins! Most questions, he rebuts by bleating on about shutting down most of the flights from "Chiyna"!

However, there is one exchange that should ensure journalist, Paula Reid from CBS News, a place in the journalistic hall of fame, if there is one. The exchange, coming after more boasts about the lives saved by shutting down China, is short, but there is only one winner. And it's not The Orange One.

> REID. What did you do with that time you bought? The argument is that you bought yourself some time. You didn't use it to prepare hospitals. You didn't use it to ramp up testing. Right now, nearly twenty million people are unemployed. Tens of thousands of Americans are dead.

Trump talks over her, saying, "You're so disgraceful. It's so disgraceful the way you say that."

REID. How is this newsreel (referring to the video) or this rant supposed to make people feel confident in an unprecedented crisis?

TRUMP. I just went over it. I just went over it. Nobody thought we should do it, but I did it. (He's talking about closing China—again.)

REID. But what did you do with the time you bought—the entire month of February?

TRUMP. What do you do when you have no case in the whole of the United States...?

REID. You had cases everywhere.

TRUMP. Excuse me. You reported it. Zero cases, zero deaths on January 17.

REID. February, you had a complete gap for the entire month of February.

TRUMP. I said in January.

REID. What did your administration do in February with the time your travel ban bought you?

TRUMP. A lot, and in fact, we'll give you a list. We did a lot. Look, look, you know you're a fake. You know that. Your whole network, the way you cover it is fake. The people are wise to you. That's why you have a lower approval rating than you've ever had before, times probably three. And when you ask...let me ask you this. Why did Biden apologise? Why did he write a letter of apology?

What? Wanker!

What makes this exchange so special is that Reid goes straight for the jugular and keeps on going. Hats off to Paula Reid—times three!

Let's face it, Captain Chaos was clearly at the end of the line when leadership skills were being handed out. He thinks leadership means being able to beat the crap out of people and shut them up when they try to tell him things he doesn't want to hear. Great!

But it also means, with a few rare exceptions, those he appoints to key White House positions are either sycophants, wimps, incompetents, or out-and-out crazies. So Dumb-Arse Don was destined from the start to balls up at every crucial moment as this country fights its way through this crisis. In other words, his arrogance and ignorance doomed him to failure before any of this even started.

"Open Up the Country"

Thursday, 16 April is another day when Trump occupies centre stage at the daily briefing. It lasts a full two hours, and there is continuing discussion about opening up the country by 1 May. Seriously? Yes, seriously. This started last week, and he continues to push his let's-all-be-at-church-on-Easter-Sunday desire.

He's even been talking about issuing an order for "a great opening," not realising, or caring, that he does not have the authority to order an opening. Strange really as he previously ignored cries to push some Republican governors to issue stay-at-home orders, saying he couldn't impose such a requirement because of "something called the Constitution."

This week is also characterised by people in a number of states beginning to protest against stay-at-home measures; and we see that even in advance of 1 May that Georgia, South Carolina, Tennessee, and Florida are opening up "essential" parts of their economies.

Apparently, in Georgia, tattoo parlours, nail salons, and bowling alleys are essential parts of the economy. Good to know!

However, people's frustrations are easy to understand as many are seeing their livelihoods and savings disappear. For many, the choice is stark: stay at home and go broke or go to work and "roll the dice."

It is difficult not to sympathise with their plight, but they are putting themselves and others at risk—all this against a backdrop of an economy under massive pressure as confirmed by an additional 5.24 million new filings for unemployment benefit bringing the total registered to a staggering twenty-two million.

It's certainly not easy, but opening up businesses again when the risk of spreading the virus continues to be high, is reckless. This is a purely politically motivated gamble, but for their sakes, I hope it pays off.

Needless to say, Wanknuts, with an eye on November's election, has been encouraging protesters, saying that some governors have gone too far in their social-distancing requirements during the pandemic. In essence, he is encouraging them to ignore the White House's own guidelines, which suggest a fourteen-day decline in new cases before relaxing any restrictions.

In spite of the relaxation of conditions in some states, not everyone is happy. Some businesses have already said "no way" and will remain closed, and a number of mayors within the states have said they will ask businesses to remain closed.

Getting Back to Work—But We Need Testing, Testing, Testing

All state governors want to see numbers coming down, but crucially, they want antibody testing to be widely available. But it's not. But why antibody testing? It is generally believed that many people have already had the virus but may not realise it; and those individuals will have the antibodies, making it unlikely they will contract the virus again.

So the theory goes, if a test proves that someone has had the virus, they would then be able/eligible to return to work without the risk of infecting anyone, and they will be at no to low risk of being reinfected.

Everybody is desperate to get back to work and back to something resembling normality, but equally (nearly) everyone is aware that it needs to be a carefully orchestrated process.

We all want tests, but can we get tested? "Yes," says Trump, but "No," says everyone who can count to ten. At different times in March, various White House representatives promised that up to twenty-seven million COVID-19 tests would be available by the end of the month.

In all, only three million were available. Bit of a gap there, chaps! When pressed on the matter, Trump says, "I cannot explain the gap. I'm hearing very good things on the ground." Whatever that means. It's amazing that he can be so dismissive of numbers that are so hugely discrepant. Don, don't you understand? There's a twenty-four-million shortfall! He simply doesn't care.

But despite all, there is some relief in the number of cases and deaths in the US. There is hope that the peak may have been reached as the numbers in the last couple of days are now flattening but are not yet on a downward trajectory.

As a reminder, the first death in the US was recorded on 29 February 2020; and one month later, on 1 April, the number rose to 5,107. Only five days later, it doubled to 10,880. Five days after that, it nearly doubled again to 20,577; and now, 19 April, eight days later, it has nearly doubled again to 40,575.

Again, it's worth reminding ourselves that each of these numbers is a person.

"Black and Brown People"

We learn that the African American and Hispanic communities are being hit the hardest by COVID-19. And a number of politicians are beginning to ask for research looking into why this is, but they don't have to look far because to cite a quote directly from "Science" (part of the AAAS[2]):

---

[2] American Association for the Advancement of Science has a history that dates back to 1848. It describes its mission to "advance science, engineering, and innovation throughout the world for the benefit of all people."

Public health researchers say the reasons are no mystery. Detailed studies of past epidemics show the same tragic pattern repeating again and again: Infectious diseases more easily take hold in groups with preexisting illnesses and who must live in crowded conditions and work next to others. Minorities also have less access to health care, and constant "weathering" from discrimination batters their health, says Sandra Crouse Quinn, a public health expert at the University of Maryland, College Park.

Science reports that Black people comprise 32 percent of Louisiana's population but a startling 70 percent of the coronavirus deaths. New York City reports that Hispanics are dying from COVID-19 at a rate of twenty-two per one hundred thousand and Black people at a rate of twenty per one hundred thousand—double the rate of White people, who are dying at a rate of ten per one hundred thousand.

These are tragic but unsurprising statistics, and yet they highlight a massive irony. When I go into a supermarket or a pharmacy, the overwhelming number of supervisors, shelf-stackers, checkout staff, and cleaners are African American or Hispanic. So the people who are dying at the highest rate in our communities are the very people who play a major role in keeping our communities functioning!

Trump Issues Ban on Immigration

Demonstrating his deep understanding and compassion, on 21 April, El Wanko issues a temporary ban on all immigration to protect American jobs.

But wait. It's not that simple. There are three things we need to know. First, the offices of the Citizenship and Immigration Services are already closed, which means naturalisation ceremonies aren't taking place anyway. Second, visa processing for tourists and workers has been suspended worldwide, and third, restrictions are in place for nonessential travel.

On top of that, refugee admissions have been halted, and the administration is already cracking down at the border by turning migrants away.

So translating the above, President Peroxide wants to make sure that people who can't come in don't come in so they can't take the jobs twenty-two million Americans don't have. The man's a genius!

This is simply Trump attempting to shift the focus away from his inept handling of the coronavirus crisis to a subject that helped him win the 2016 election while simultaneously feeding red meat to his base.

By way of addendum, Trump's original objective was to impose a sixty-day ban on all immigration. But following pressure from the agricultural sector, which needed temporary farmworkers, he relaxed the "all immigration" element of the ban, so it was all a meaningless exercise.

Hydroxychloroquine—Let the Fun Begin

This is an absolute beauty and another great example of how to act when you have no idea of what you're doing, especially when you have no understanding of the problems your country is facing.

Since early April, Doctor Trump has been extoling the virtues of a drug called Hydroxychloroquine[3] as a treatment for COVID-19 patients. He has been actively supported by Fox, who have relentlessly pushed its use as a treatment. But it takes good ole' Trumpy a while to get used to the name. At first, he calls it "hydroxy-chloro-chloroquine." How sweet!

---

[3] Hydroxychloroquine is used in the treatment of lupus, malaria, and arthritis. (Lupus is a long-term autoimmune disease in which the body's immune system becomes hyperactive and attacks normal, healthy tissue. Symptoms include inflammation, swelling, and damage to the joints, skin, kidneys, blood, heart, and lungs.)

Actually, there is nothing sweet about it. He is totally unqualified to talk on the subject. The medical profession is saying trials are needed first. Trials? Screw that! Our snake-oil seller tells us all that we should try it, asking, "What have you got to lose?" Well, apart from your life, not much, I suppose.

Next comes what I think is the genuinely smart part of his pleading. It is 100 percent cynical but clever, nonetheless.

Standing at the podium at a subsequent Shite House virus briefing, he becomes serious and intense. He lowers his voice to a whisper and says that if we try hydroxychloroquine, "it will be wonderful. It'll be so beautiful. It'll be like a gift from heaven."

I was struck by his choice of words and the theatre of his performance, so I googled "it'll be wonderful…so beautiful…" Guess what? I found that a popular singer songwriter of Christian music called Natalie Grant has a successful song called "Isn't He (This Jesus)," the opening words of which are "So wonderful, so beautiful." Trump is definitely an arsehole, but he knows his evangelicals!

As of 22 April, the hydroxy story seems to have been put to bed. Results of drug trials, albeit limited, in France, Sweden, and Brazil do not show it to be the saviour. In fact, it may even increase the mortality rate. Sorry, Don, you'll have to find a new shiny object. He was very quiet on the matter today.

But a subject on which he is not so quiet is opening up the country, specifically Georgia, where Republican governor Brian Kemp, a born-again Trump-pleaser, decided to open up parts of the state.

Trump is so happy that he calls Kemp to congratulate him, but the medics in the task force team are not happy and persuade Trump to step back from his support—which he does by saying the opening was too soon! What leadership! Failing by example.

More Unemployed

23 April: Today we learn that a further 4.4 million people registered for unemployment, bringing the total to nearly 26.5 million. It's difficult to comprehend these numbers, but they bring

home just how serious a situation we are in and give grave cause for concern for the future, especially for those who are already desperately in need of money.

A number of people have expressed a feeling of helplessness, with no job, no prospects, and no sign of things changing anytime soon. Worldwide COVID-19 cases are now 2.63 million, and deaths are 18,466. In the US, 849,000 cases and 47,659 dead.

In May 2019, the Federal Reserve conducted a survey, which showed almost 40 percent of American adults wouldn't be able to cover a $400 emergency with cash, savings, or a credit-card charge that they could quickly pay off.

So how are those people coping today? Simple. They're not. There are huge queues at food banks all over the country. In many places, people are waiting in line for hours.

It's the same in France, England, Italy. You name it. Even in Thailand, which has a population of seventy million, there are twenty-seven million (nearly 40 percent of the population) queuing for food!

By the way, I understand that in Thai "Donald Trump" translates as "Phat Phuk." Who knew?

Disinfectant—The COVID Cure!

Having had to kick his hydroxy plans into touch, Trump now comes up with another beauty. He suggests at today's White House coronavirus task force briefing that we should *inject ourselves with disinfectant*!

Following a presentation on how the virus behaves in certain environments and its reaction to chemicals, Trump spontaneously comes up with a cure, giving the impression he has already discussed it with task force coordinator, Dr. Deborah Birx, which he has not. This is what he says:

> So supposing we hit the body with a tremendous—whether it's ultraviolet or just very powerful light. I think you [turning to Birx] said

that hasn't been checked, but you're going to test it. And then I said supposing you brought the light inside of the body, which you can do either through the skin or in some other way. And I think you said you're going to test that too. Sounds interesting.

Yes, it does sound interesting—and lethal too.

And then I see the disinfectant where it knocks it out in a minute. One minute. [He's referring to comments of the previous speaker.] And is there a way we can do something like that by injection inside or almost a cleaning? So it'd be interesting to check that.

He then asks Birx whether she has ever heard of using "the heat and the light" to treat viruses. "Not as a treatment," Birx says. "I mean, certainly, fever is a good thing. When you have a fever, it helps your body respond. But I've not seen heat or light."

I should add here that while President Crapspeak is positing his theory, Birx is sitting stage left, looking totally horror-struck. When Trump started, she was looking at him, but as he revealed his cunning plan, she looked down with her hands clasped tightly together. You could almost hear her thinking, *Fuuuuuuuck!*

And this, ladies and gentlemen, is the leader of the Free World! Trump is always the first to tell everyone how smart he is. Well, he's not smart. He's not even smart enough to realise how stupid he is.

C'mon, Captain Clorox!

What a day yesterday was. Well done, Domestos Don! I absolutely loved it! He…is…such…a…tit! He has now proved to the world beyond any shadow of doubt that he really is that stupid—even parts of Fox were saying "WTF?" But not all parts.

Fox News Primetime (one of Ajax Man's favourites) ignores the subject completely.

But a column in *Breitbart News* runs a headline defending Trump, "Fact Check: No, Trump Didn't Propose Injecting People with Disinfectant." *Breitbart* later retracts the "fact check," saying the column "should have been framed as an opinion piece."

But what brought about Brillo Boy's balls up in the first place? It was pure ego. One of the reasons he became a fixture at the daily briefings was because they had proved a success, with experts sharing useful coronavirus information.

But as we know, Trump, being the camera-loving narcissistic wanknut he is, does not like others being in the limelight; so Mr. Muscle puts himself front and centre and uses the opportunity to do some free campaigning, as well as to highlight his total lack of knowledge on all matters medical, and everything else for that matter.

Let's hope his self-obsessive behaviour will result in a swing in the "tide" of public opinion to the Democrats and that all chances of his being reelected "vanish" in a "flash!"

COVID-19 Remains Unrelenting

As we close in on the end of the month, we have seen yet more milestones passed. Total deaths worldwide now exceed two hundred thousand; and yesterday, cases broke through the three-million mark, having passed one million at the beginning of the month and two million only twelve days ago. USA cases are now over one million and deaths are just shy of sixty thousand.

We see that some twenty-four states (and that number is rising rapidly) are set to relax certain restrictions this week. I think it may prove to be too much too soon, but the pressure on governors is increasing by the day and is absolutely not helped by Trump adding fuel to the fire of frustration by breaking from public-health guidelines, saying America should return to work. He again shows a total lack of leadership.

Currently, the US is behaving more like fifty countries rather than fifty states. Indeed, many states are already like countries (California has a 39.4 million population and is the fifth largest economy in the world; Texas, 29.4 million population; Florida, 21.7 million; New York, 19.3 million), so the job is not an easy one. But Trump does nothing to bring people together.

In fact, quite the opposite. He says the governor of Michigan, Gretchen Whitmer, should "do a deal" with armed protesters who want an end to the lockdown order. But she says this is not a political problem over which a deal can be done. This is about people's lives. She's very smart and committed, and these are not easy days for her.

For a bit of perspective, China, New Zealand, Germany, Spain, France, and Singapore have all opened up parts of their economies; and China, Germany, and Singapore have already seen a subsequent uptick in new cases. This is not unexpected and needs to be managed. It also provides valuable lessons to others in the management of secondary spikes.

So How Is Trump Doing?

A poll published today, 29 April, asks about Trump's handling of the crisis. It shows 55 percent pleased, 45 percent not pleased. I don't get it! How can so many people be pleased?

There seem to be a few reasons. Some support Trump regardless; others are Fox fannies. Others believe the Democrats are deliberately overplaying the seriousness of COVID-19, and of course, there are groups of dueling banjo players whose brothers are also their uncles. Oh yes, and Trump's reaction to the poll? "It's fake, fake. It's totally fake!" He clearly thinks he's doing better.

But the "funniest" thing of the day comes thanks to the bollocks uttered by none other than Jared Kushner, knower of nothing and all-round bloody idiot.

He appears on Fox, saying, "We are on the other side of the medical aspect of this, and I think that we have achieved all of the different milestones that are needed. The federal government rose to the challenge, and this is a great success story. And I think that that's really, you know, what needs to be told."

Well done, Brainless. The milestones you "achieved" are COVID-19 cases in excess of one million, more than sixty thousand deaths, and twenty-six million unemployed. Great achievement, you arse. Whatever happened to the "nearly zero" forecast by that other idiot?

You and your lot are nothing more than a bunch of self-interested failures who feed on the frustrations and hopes of others. Shame on you. But let's not forget. This situation would never have arisen if politicians everywhere had been more honest in the first place.

We should demand more of those who represent us. To quote the late senator John McCain, "We are better than this."

More Registered Unemployed, but the Dow Improves

So the month draws to a close. A further 3.8 million register for unemployment benefit. The number registering is declining week by week, but the new additions bring the total to an unimaginable thirty million. And it's not over yet, even though we have already reached the highest rate of unemployment since 1948, when data collection began.

But let's end the month with some good news. First, the Dow started the month at 20,943 and climbed an impressive 3,392 points to close the month at 24,335; and second, Trump says he has "done a spectacular job in handling the virus"! That's a relief because I thought he was screwing it up.

May 2020

Opening Too Soon?

I mentioned that twenty-four states were gearing up to relax some restrictions and that the number was rising. Well, that number is now at forty-one and expected to rise further still; but none have met two key White House guidelines for opening—namely, there must be fourteen consecutive days of declining new infections and adequate testing must be in place.

This has given rise to a revision of the number of expected deaths. According to one of the models used by the White House, projected deaths in the US by the end of August will increase to 134,000 from 72,500, but no surprise there as deaths in the US today are already over 70,000 and look likely to be above 100,000 by the beginning of June. In fact, by the end of August, we will see deaths reach 189,000.

Many states have unquestionably been premature in relaxing some of their measures and are not helped by the unwillingness of some individuals to wear masks. Indeed, in Michigan, a security guard is shot dead by someone refusing to wear a mask when asked to do so. This is America!

Ohio reverses an order that masks should be worn, as does Oklahoma City because of such a strong negative public reaction. Hard to believe but true.

But how does this bode for the future? From today's perspective, not well. People all over the country are fed up, angry, and frustrated because they can't get back to work. Many have reached the point where "enough is enough."

Understandable, but they're still wrong. So what is missing? First and foremost, it's leadership, which sadly remains absent. The only thing Captain Cretin cares about is getting reelected, and there is no limit to the number of American lives lost that he will tolerate to achieve that.

Despite all, however, a number of the states that are opening are doing so on a gradual basis and are maintaining the requirement of social distancing. So if people act responsibly, second spikes should be containable. Fingers crossed!

Unemployment Numbers—Getting Worse, and It's Still Not Over

After last week's sixth consecutive rise in those filing for unemployment for the first week, a report on Thursday, 7 May, shows that another 3.2 million people filed for the first time last week, bringing the total number of jobs lost in the last seven weeks to at least 33.5 million! The numbers may be coming down week by week, but the total continues to rise.

As we live through this day by day, I think we become somewhat inured to what is happening, but then our focus is on the light on the other side rather than what is actually happening. It's easier to cope that way.

We are living through a tragedy that will change all our lives forever. At least, I hope it does, and I hope we become better for it.

Just as a reminder of reality, today, Friday, 8 May, COVID-19 cases worldwide top 4,000,000 and deaths 275,000. This compares with 1,500,000 cases and 88,000 deaths only one month earlier. Over the same period, cases in the US rise from 435,000 to 1,300,000 million and deaths from 14,800 to 78,600.

It's Saturday, 9 May, and it snowed today in New York! Seems appropriate somehow.

What's His Game?

Trump had an unbelievable opportunity to bring the country together to help the country understand why it was important to stay at home, but he squandered it. Don't bother asking yourself why. It's easy to say Trump has no understanding of the importance of testing and tracing, but he understands it fully.

He understands that more tests mean more new cases, and that's not good! Keep the numbers as low as possible. Given his objectives, qualities such as leadership and empathy are unnecessary, which is just as well as he is devoid of them anyway.

By contrast, New York state governor Cuomo gives daily press conferences in which he explains what's happening, what the issues are, and what lies ahead. It's about the facts, and unlike Trump, he realises the importance of testing and tracing.

But be in no doubt, New Yorkers are just as fed up, angry, and frustrated as anyone else in the country; but Cuomo's facts-based approach has people pulling together and beats Trump's nonsense any day—so far, at least.

Trump continues to urge states to open up their economies, even though in many instances, new cases are still on the rise; and by 11 May, almost all states have relaxed some restrictions.

In recent days, however, there has been a bit of a wake-up call at the Shite House as a couple of staff tested positive for the virus. It is widely reported that Trump is not happy and is refusing to meet with anyone who is not COVID-clear.

He was asked if this will change his thinking on returning to work, but he continues to push for states to open up and to downplay the importance of testing and tracing.

Divide and Rule—Make It Partisan

We can talk all day about how the Portly Pres is uncaring and unfeeling, but what's the point? Being unfeeling is what defines him. He has no sense of decency nor honesty and is totally without scruples, and that's why he may very well get reelected.

He does two things successfully. His daily bleating that "Chiyna" is to blame resonates with his base, so none of this is his fault. Forget that he had originally praised China for their handling of the situation and that he did bugger all during the whole of February. None of that matters. His base has its red meat, and they're happy.

He also manages to turn the appalling death toll into the fault of the Democrats. He is effectively saying all he wants is for the country to get back to work, but the Democratic states are holding back because they don't care about the economy. And they want to him to lose the election.

Blaming the Democrats resonates well with many of the newly unemployed who look to Trump to get them back to work, and the Democrats are feeling the pressure. So Trump is now the hero, and the Democrats are the villains. Amazing.

We still have a long way to go with this. But at the moment, Democrats are on the back foot, and they need to do something about it.

Trump Quote for the Day

14 May: Trump doesn't like the fact testing for coronavirus tells you how many cases there are and says, "If we didn't do any testing, we would have very few cases."

Not quite, Sherlock!

Maybe Trump Has Other Worries…

Apart from the political games he plays to gain reelection, there may well be something else that is not being widely reported that motivates his dismissive attitude to testing and tracing, and that's money—his money—or perhaps the lack of it!

He boasts being worth $10 billion. But according to *Forbes Magazine*, his pre-coronavirus net worth was $3.1 billion. In March 2020, Forbes reduced its estimate to $2.1 billion, but I wouldn't be surprised if it were even lower.

None of his properties or other businesses are generating income at the moment, but he still has costs. Maybe that's why he's so keen to see a high stock market and a return to work. Trump lies about absolutely everything, but whilst he may not react to all criticism, he always fights back when his alleged wealth is questioned.

Trump has long been suspected of dodgy dealings. He has a string of business failures behind him, and he's been bankrupt several times. There have been suspicions raised about his direct involvement with money laundering on property transactions, where other players have included Deutsche Bank and shady rich Russians.

I would not be at all surprised to learn that he's up to his neck in debt in Russia, probably unable to service the interest and repayment costs and, on a net basis, is worth next to shag all.[4] The problem for him this time may be quite different. Normally, Captain Crook either refuses to pay or takes people to court. Good luck doing that if you owe the Russians, matey!

Trump's Ego and Alter Ego

We know Trump lies about absolutely everything all the time, but next to his (lack of) wealth, another favourite subject is women and how they fall at his feet. He has made multiple calls to journalists on these subjects while posing as a Trump publicist, saying what a great guy he is and how much money he's got.

He often used the names "John Miller" or "John Barron." In the 1980s, in a John Barron call to Jonathan Greenberg, then of *Forbes Magazine*, he wanted to get his name on the first-ever *Forbes* 400 list, saying Trump's father had transferred assets to him, which was a lie. Trump/Barron was worth a maximum of $5 million at the time but persuaded *Forbes* he was worth $100 million and got on the list.

---

[4] Back in 2006, Trump filed a lawsuit against author Timothy O'Brien for $5 billion because O'Brien said Trump's net worth was no more than $250 million. The case was kicked out of court. At that time, Trump was claiming to be worth between $5 billion and $6 billion.

In another John Barron example, he told *People* magazine in 1991 that Trump was dumping his girlfriend, Marla Maples (he was later to marry her in 1993), for another woman. The reporter who spoke with "Barron" knew immediately it was Trump and played a recording of the call to Maples.

She also recognised it as Trump's voice and was not a happy bunny. Trump later admitted it was him and apologised to the magazine. However, when he was asked about this again in 2016, he denied it.

Aside from Barron and Miller, he has also shown his feminine side and posed as a Carolin Gallego, secretary to the wonderful and amazing Donald Trump. "She" wrote in response to a *New York Magazine* article, bemoaning Trump's treatment of women. "I do not believe any man in America gets more calls from women wanting to see him, meet him, or go out with him. The most beautiful women, the most successful women—all women love Donald Trump." How's that for a display of insecurity?

Needless to say, no traces of Barron, Miller, or Gallego have ever been tracked down, but playing with the letters of Carolin Gallego, I see it's an anagram of "one call girl ago" and "a call girl gone." Food for thought?

Back to the Story—The Virus Is History!

Trump becomes bolder. On Friday, 15 May, he declares, "Vaccine or no vaccine, we're back," and, once again, seems to diminish the virulence of COVID-19. He's pushing hard on his back-to-work message, and there is some reporting that privately he's even challenging the number of deaths reported.

He continues not to wear a mask and to encourage disruptive behaviour—all this despite the fact he's petrified of being near anyone who hasn't been tested in the last five minutes or who hasn't had bleach shoved up their rear end. And his fans love him for it!

Naturally, Dopey Don Jr. and his witless brother, Eric—together known as Tweedledumb and Tweedledumber[5]—don't want to miss out on any of the fun. Tweedledumb goes off at a complete tangent and tweets about recent allegations that Joe Biden had touched women inappropriately and even suggests Biden is a paedophile. What a lowlife he is.

He later says he was joking but that Biden should "stop the unwanted touching and keep his hands to himself." Meanwhile, Tweedledumber appears on Fox News, claiming the Democrats are using the pandemic, which has killed nearly ninety thousand in the country, for political gain. Daddy must be very proud.

Hydroxychloroquine Returns!

18 May: We all thought Trump was finished with promoting hydroxychloroquine, the lupus and malaria drug, but we are wrong—very wrong! Trump still sees it as a coronavirus prophylactic and announces today he is actually taking it and has been for about ten days!

Amazing—he takes a drug that medics say he shouldn't and yet still refuses to wear a mask, when medics say he should. What a genius, but at least he won't get lupus or malaria. Maybe he owns shares in Sanofi, the French company producing the drug.

Dow Jones Index Up

Still on 18 May, the Dow has its best day since the beginning of April and closes at 24,597, up 912 points. This is on the news that Moderna, a US biotech company, reported positive "phase 1" results for a potential coronavirus vaccine. The company says that after two doses, all forty-five trial participants had developed coronavirus antibodies.

---

[5] Borrowed from Tweedledum and Tweedledee, characters in an English nursery rhyme and in Lewis Carroll's book *Through the Looking-Glass, and What Alice Found There.*

This timeline is well ahead of the twelve to eighteen months we were earlier told to expect, which is encouraging, but forty-five participants seem to be a pretty small sample. Anyway, good news is good news, and that's a big jump in the Dow.

One Hundred Thousand Coronavirus Deaths in the US

There is a lot of tension at the moment as the death toll marches inexorably to 100,000. The official numbers are regarded as those produced by Johns Hopkins University, but on 25 May, *The New York Times* reported that the death toll was probably already 130,000 if you include "people who had the virus but weren't diagnosed, as well as those who died for indirect reasons, such as delaying medical treatment for other illnesses."

This is a truly sad moment and gives everyone pause for reflection on reaching this tragic landmark. These are all people who have left behind family and friends.

Everyone? Did I say it gives everyone pause for reflection? What I meant to say was everyone except one person. You know who I mean: the guy who wants to inject himself with bleach, the guy who said a couple of years ago that we should look into detonating a nuclear bomb in the middle of a hurricane. Great idea. A radioactive hurricane!

Trump says nothing about the 100,000 deaths. His silence on such a sad milestone is deafening; and his lack of response is noted on all the TV news stations, bar one. But finally, twenty-four hours later, he tweets a message of condolence. What a hero!

"Mail-In Ballots"—A Twit on Twitter

Although the election is not until November, the subject of voting by mail is a hot discussion topic. Trump is completely against it as there is some evidence that Democrats fare better with mail-in ballots.

So in a tweet on 26 May, Trump says that mail-in ballots are substantially fraudulent, that mail boxes will be robbed, that ballots will be illegally printed and fraudulently signed. Of course, none of this is true, and any historical evidence of fraud and skullduggery is scant, at best.[6]

However, what separates this tweet from all others is that for the first time, Twitter added a "fact-check label" to the tweet, saying, "Get the facts about mail-in ballots," indicating Trump was not honest. Imagine that!

Fatty seems to forget that after the 2016 election, he was so frustrated Hillary won the popular vote by more than 2.8 million that in May 2017, he set up a commission gloriously named "The Presidential Advisory Commission on Election Integrity" to investigate voting fraud. He bleated that between three million and five million ballots had been cast by illegal immigrants, so Hillary did not win the popular vote. So there!

Even though the commission was headed by VP Pence, it was disbanded after eight months with no evidence found to substantiate the claims of the petulant Chubby Chump. Through a Shite House statement, Chubby blamed the lack of findings on "many states' refusal to turn over information, as well as legal disputes." This is totally untrue.

Trump is now at war with Twitter; and, on 27 May, signs an executive order aimed at removing protection that social media companies have against being sued by users. But Twitter is not backing down.

The following day, Trump posts two tweets about violence in Minneapolis, and both are slapped with what Twitter calls a "public interest notice," flagging the post as glorifying violence. This means the tweets are not removed but are hidden behind a notice that says, "This tweet violated the Twitter rules about glorifying violence."

So to read the tweets, you first need to click on the notice. I don't know where this will end up, but I like it so far! Trump, I'm

---

[6] This turns out to be what will become the beginning of Trump's "big lie," saying that the election he will later lose to Biden was stolen.

sure, loves it as it is yet another distraction, but this subject is far from closed.

George Floyd: 14 October 1973–25 May 2020

George Floyd's death at the hands of Minneapolis police officers on 25 May 2020 is a day in the time of COVID-19 that will live in world history. Floyd is arrested by police and placed facedown on the ground with his hands cuffed behind his back.

Four police officers are involved with the arrest, three holding him down and one standing in front of Floyd. George Floyd is not resisting, nor is he struggling to break free. It is therefore beyond belief that one officer, Derek Chauvin, a nineteen-year police veteran, has his knee on Floyd's neck, keeping him pinned to the ground. Another has his knee in his back, and for good measure, a third is holding his legs. George Floyd is completely immobilised.

Despite having their suspect fully within their control, the police do nothing to reflect that. Instead, Chauvin keeps his knee on Floyd's neck and even increases the pressure. Floyd repeatedly says, "I can't breathe." He even calls for his deceased mother, and he says, "I'm dying." He was right. George Floyd dies facedown in the road with Chauvin's knee on his neck.

In total, he is on the ground for eight minutes and forty-six seconds, and for the last two minutes and fifty-three seconds, the police cannot feel a pulse. Yet Chauvin does not remove his knee, nor does he ease up on the pressure he's applying to George Floyd's neck. Chauvin even ignores members of the public who implore the police to let him breathe.

George Floyd's death gives rise to daily protest marches in over 130 cities and towns throughout the country. Many cities, including New York, suffer at the hands of looters; and fires are set, destroying property and police cars. Only a few blocks from where we live, shop fronts were destroyed, and a police car was set on fire.

Trump's solution to the violence is to add more fuel to the fire. On 29 May, he tweets "When the looting starts, the shooting starts."This repeats what the Miami chief of police said during the race riots there in 1967. Twitter flags Trump's tweet.

Violence and looting must be condemned, and I hope that those responsible are caught and punished. But for the record, the majority of marches are peaceful, and marchers are people of all races.

George Floyd's death has not only touched the hearts of most Americans, it has touched the hearts of people around the world with protest marches taking place throughout Europe, in Canada, Brazil, Argentina, Australia—the list goes on.

But the deaths of Black men caused by White policemen in this country is not new. It's common and has a long history, as is the fact that hardly any police officer ever gets indicted, let alone convicted. That is not to say that the police are at fault in every case—they're not. But racism is part of everyday society in the US.

Kareem Abdul-Jabbar, a basketball legend, writes in the *Los Angeles Times*, "African Americans have been living in a burning building for many years, choking on the smoke as the flames burn closer and closer. Racism in America is like dust in the air. It seems invisible—even if you're choking on it—until you let the sun in. Then you see it's everywhere."

Maybe everyone can hope that the death of George Floyd can be a catalyst for movement towards a positive change. We can always hope.

Fortress White House

The death of George Floyd presents Trump with another opportunity to demonstrate leadership and bring the country together. Sadly but predictably, it is yet another opportunity he doesn't see or, perhaps even worse, ignores.

As demonstrations take place near the Shite House on Friday, 29 May, the intrepid leader decides he will be safer if he takes refuge in a bunker five stories below ground! He later denies he was taking refuge in the bunker; instead, he was "inspecting it." Of course you were, Donny dear.

And just to prove Donny-Wonny is not afraid of anyone, he has an eight-foot fence erected around the perimeter of the White House and calls in the National Guard to "defend" him. What a hapless fool he is.

June 2020

Time to Praise the Lord

On the first day of June, with protests outside the White House, Trump stands in the Rose Garden and says that disturbances should be handled by deploying the military! He then confirms how deluded he is by telling everyone he is the "president of law and order."

He finishes by saying, "I am going to pay my respects to a very, very special place," and so proceeds to walk with a number of his aides to a damaged St. John's Church for a photo opportunity where he will pose with a Bible in his hand. The Bible is carried by his daughter, and I can just imagine the conversation between them:

"Ivanka, pass me the elbib."

"The what?"

"The elbib."

"What elbib?"

"That book you're holding, the elbib."

"Oh, you mean the Bible."

"But is says elbib."

"You're reading it upside down, Dad."

"Oh really? Yeah, I knew that."

So there he stands there, Bible in hand, looking like the prat he is. He holds it like it might blow up in his hands. Shame it didn't.

He is criticised and ridiculed for his actions, especially as the crowd in Lafayette Square near the White House before his "walk for fame" were pushed, punched, flash-banged, and tear gassed out of the way. Classy stuff!

I can see St. John's Church becoming another photography hotspot just as Abbey Road in London did after The Beatles were photographed there for an album cover in 1969. Not quite the same, though.

Monday, 8 June 2020: New York Partially Reopens

After seventy-seven days of lockdown and one hundred days since the first case in New York was identified, some businesses in Manhattan reopen today, but we are still a long way from being able to walk the streets without masks or sit in our favourite restaurants to enjoy a meal with friends and family.

We have been under an 8:00 p.m. to 5:00 a.m. curfew for a few days, but that was lifted yesterday—so a bit more good news. However, Manhattan is battered and bruised. Its once-bustling streets have been reduced to rows of boarded-up shops and build-ings. It's a mess. It looks derelict, and it's depressing.

COVID Raises Its Ugly Head Again

Only a few days ago, I expressed a hope that coronavirus would not come back as states open up. Well, it's back. Some eigh-teen states are seeing an increase in cases. Testing has increased, so more cases are showing up. But hospitalisations are also on the up, which is more telling. Many states are keeping a watchful eye on developments, as concerns are they may need to close down again.

The uptick in numbers is due to a mixture of reasons. Some states opened too early. Some gathering places, such as beaches for example, were not closed soon enough. There was the celebration of spring break, the celebration of Memorial Day, and, of course, demonstrations following the death of George Floyd.

There are real fears that the virus will come back with a ven-geance. A forecast yesterday, 10 June, projects a further 100,000 deaths in the US before the end of September. The current death total stands at 112,000, and today the US broke through the 2 million case barrier. The world totals are 7.4 million cases and more than 400,000 deaths. These numbers never cease to shock.

And talking of numbers, the Dow has seen strong growth recently. Since the middle of May to 8 June, the Dow added a staggering 4,000-plus points and reached 27,570. Pundits point to its success being due to continued support from the Federal Reserve's buying government and corporate bonds and investors buying into the future. Investors appear to be less concerned with where we are today but more where we will be later now that the economy moves to open.

However, on 10 June, the chairman of the Fed, Jerome Powell, warns that recovery may be slower than hoped. On 11 June, the Dow closes a long way down at 25,100.

Trump's Rally Doesn't Really Rally

For some time, President Chump has been hailing an upcoming rally in Tulsa, Oklahoma, as a signal of a return to normality. He has long said that he wants to see people shoulder to shoulder in an indoor arena, despite the risks.

The scheduled rally date is 19 June, but the problem with that is that it happens to coincide with what is known as "Juneteenth," the oldest known celebration honouring the end of slavery in the US on 19 June 1865.

Add to that, ninety-nine years ago on 31 May and 1 June, White mobs attacked Black residents, their homes, and businesses in Tulsa—destroying thirty-five blocks and leaving ten thousand Blacks homeless. The number of deaths has never been confirmed, but estimates vary between as many as 150 to 300.

So it comes as no surprise that the Black community strongly opposes the choice of date and location of the rally. It is seen by many as being an overtly racist move by Trump. Somewhat surprisingly, Trump agrees to change the date to one day later, 20 June. He is excited at the prospect of another rally and boasts that one million people have applied for tickets to the event.

The arena chosen has a capacity of only 20,000, so arrangements are made for Trump and Mike Pence to address an anticipated overflow crowd of 40,000 outside the arena so no one will be disappointed and everyone will get a chance to see Fatman and Blobbin.

But wait! Where is everybody? The attendance is so poor that the overflow address is cancelled, and inside the arena, the crowd is only 6,500. Bit of a shortfall there, matey! A disaster for Trump but a pleasure to witness.

I'm sure there are a number of reasons why this is such a failure, among which may be that many people are indeed worried about contracting the virus.

Others may have been put off by Trump talking about how protesters will be dealt with and so have stayed away. Whatever the reasons, I doubt the same mistakes will be made again, so I enjoy the moment but hold back on any celebration.

Early Openers Pay the Price

Where will this end? Trump's refusal to acknowledge the seriousness of coronavirus and the importance of testing and wearing masks has impacted the behaviour of governors in a number of states. A good example is Arizona (population 7.3 million), which sees a huge spike in cases and hospitalisations since reopening in mid-May.

To make matters worse, an increasing number of younger people are diagnosed with the virus. Pro-Trump governor, Doug Ducey, is now allowing county leaders in the state to impose mask-wearing, but despite strong medical advice, he still refuses to make it a statewide order. It's appalling to realise that people are dying because of the politics and egos of others.

Other good examples of how not to do things are in more highly populated states like Florida (21.7 million) and Texas (29.4 million), both of which also begin reopening around mid-May.

Governor Ron DeSantis of Florida declares as early as the beginning of May that all is well and the media is full of "doom and gloom." Daily cases then were 350. Today, 22 June, the daily cases are 3,500 with a total of 77,500. Deaths at opening were 1,900 and are now 3,175. The numbers are not looking good.

Governor Greg Abbott of Texas, another head-up-his-arse governor, has seen a massive increase in cases since reopening, and there are no indications of a slowdown. Total cases are currently 125,000, but an unbelievable 30,000 of those have been within the last week!

Abbott, who says, "Texans don't like being told what to do," confirms there will be no return to an economic lockdown and limits public gatherings to 100, down from 500. WTF? Oh yes, and he has urged people to stay at home. Let's hope they do because right now, Texas intensive care units have a 97 percent occupancy rate.

Another Rally

Two days after the failed rally in Tulsa, Trump's next effort is in Phoenix, Arizona; but this time, he holds it in a church with a capacity of three thousand. So it's not so much a rally, a small gathering rather. Anyway, at least the place is full, so ten out of ten for attendance but zero for substance.

Talking of Which, Mike Pence

Friday, 26 June, the White House holds a medical team briefing for the first time in two months. Trump is not there, just Pence and the medics. Pence, being the good churchgoing Christian he is, opens with "All fifty states across this territory are opening up safely and responsibly." Safely? Responsibly? What about the numbers?

In saying that, he is repeating Trump's deluded outpourings and reinforcing the widening divide in the country about the progress and management of COVID-19. Why doesn't anybody say and do things that bring people together?

Anyway, Pence knows that COVID "across this territory" is on the rise in thirty-three states. Fourteen of the thirty-three have either reversed or paused their plans for opening, and in seven states, hospitalisations are at record levels.

So much for the notion that states are "opening safely and responsibly." Pence is a joke, and he too is not worthy of the position he holds.

We are all suffering from COVID fatigue, and things are getting worse, not better in many parts of the country. But again, I lay much of the blame at Trump's feet. This is so demoralising.

It is undeniable that with good leadership, the death toll would be far lower, and the country would be on its way to a more normal way of life. Trump really doesn't give a shit about anything other than his reelection.

A real tragedy is that Trump will never be held to account for the deaths he has caused. Of course, we cannot judge what that number is but must be in the thousands. He is an utter disgrace.

July 2020

More Milestones to Shame

It's 8 July, and today the US reaches three million cases out of twelve million worldwide and accounts for 132,000 deaths out of the world's 545,000. Things are just not getting any better. Dr. Anthony Fauci, the leading US infectious diseases expert, says we are not on top of things and that we are "knee-deep" in problems.

However, the Pink Porker disagrees, saying that the death rate is falling, which is true, and that in three to four weeks, "we'll be in good shape," which is bollocks.

It is indeed good to see the death rate falling, and that is partly to do with doctors knowing more about the virus and how to treat patients and partly because hospitals have not been under pressure with ICU beds at capacity. However, that's very likely to change, and we will almost certainly see in three to four weeks that things are worse, not better.

Hospitalisations are sharply on the rise, most notably in Texas, California, Florida, Arizona, and Georgia. At the end of June, after daily record cases in Arizona, Governor Doug Ducey reversed all relaxation measures and ordered all bars, gyms, cinemas, theatres, and water parks closed for thirty days. It's a step in the right direction, but I doubt it will be enough.

The governors of Florida and Texas have boxed themselves into a corner. They have gone so far down the political road of fools that they have made it difficult to put the brakes on, let alone turn back.

California, despite being a Democratic state, is seeing all its good early work being undone. In less than a month, new cases have more than doubled to over 300,000 and deaths are rising to record levels every day. What a bunch of irresponsible idiots.

Trump Continues to Flounder

Trump seems to have gone completely off his rocker. He bounces from one idiot statement to the next, offering no solutions, only attributing blame. He says that it's a good thing the US leads the world in COVID-19 cases and that he views it as a badge of honour. Unbelievable!

He's also fallen out with Dr. Fauci because of his comments on the spread of the virus. Basically, Fauci is saying it's a mess and that we are nowhere near the end of our troubles. What may have got under Trump's skin was that Fauci contradicted him by saying, "I don't think you can say we're doing great. I mean, we're just not." Trump now says Fauci "made a lot of mistakes" and can't be relied on because of the errors he made at the beginning.

Then, White House staff release a memo to members of the media with a long list of "Fauci's mistakes," but the bait is not taken and no one publishes the list—not even Fox!

Houston, We've Got a Problem!

What a mess in Texas. As at 13 July, total cases have doubled to 274,000 in just eighteen days. "The more you test, the more cases you find," says Trump again. Duh! But hospitalisations today are 10,500, which is more than double the number over the same eighteen-day period. Deaths are also up by over one thousand—accounting for 33 percent of all deaths in less than three weeks.

Many people blame Governor Greg Abbott for opening too soon. Even though the opening of restaurants, bars, gyms, etc. was in stages, it was still too quick. It made Texans feel it was all over. Social distancing was thrown out of the window, along with the masks. Any belief that all would soon be back to normal was quickly understood to be no more than a fanciful notion.

Texans are now deeper in the mire than they were before, and the governor finally hits the pause button on 25 June. But he is not reversing any of the measures already taken; he's just putting further openings on hold.

However, having previously overturned orders by Democratic mayors that people should wear masks, he now says everybody should wear a mask—great leadership. But look at his role model. His problems are far from over.

If Texas Is a Mess, Florida Is a Basket Case

You have good governors; you have bad governors. And then you have Ron DeSantis. Through his leadership, DeSantis ensures Florida goes from bad to worse and now worst. I mentioned that by 22 June, cases statewide were 77,500. well, by 30 June, they nearly double to 150,000, and fifteen days later, they do indeed double to 300,000!

And just to show it's not all about test numbers, deaths in Florida on 22 June were 3,175; by 30 June 3,500; and by 15 July, 4,500—still averaging 500 per week. And deaths are what tell the real story. The seven-day moving average for deaths is 15 June 32; 30 June 38; 15 July 90.

DeSantis still says all is OK as he banks on the fact that there a lot of younger victims and that they "aren't affected so badly." True, but they better not mix with "older" people. By 16 July, Florida confirms that ICU beds in a number of hospitals are at full capacity. But don't worry, y'all. DeSantis says it's OK.

Some Random Observations

Jeff Sessions, former attorney general appointed by Trump but later fired for recusing himself from the investigation into Russia's interference into the 2016 election, recently lost the

Alabama Senate race to Trump's preferred candidate, a dickhead named Tommy Tuberville.

Tommy is a former American football coach and avid Trumper. He loves him so much he actually said, "I do believe today that God sent Donald Trump to us." I'm not sure if that's proof that God does exist or does not!

A niece of Trump, Mary Trump, who is fifty-five and has a doctoral degree in clinical psychology, has just written a book about Trump entitled *Too Much and Never Enough: How My Family Created the World's Most Dangerous Man*.

She writes that for Uncle Don, "nothing is ever enough" and that he exhibits all the characteristics of a narcissist, saying, "This is far beyond garden-variety narcissism." She says, "Donald is not simply weak. His ego is a fragile thing that must be bolstered every moment because he knows deep down that he is nothing of what he claims to be."

In another part of the book, she refers to him as a sociopath. Agreed! She also says he was afraid of failing his SAT test (a standardised test widely used for college admissions), so he paid someone to take the test for him. Of course, he denies it, which, by definition, makes it true!

A number of recent polls show variously that Trump is not doing well in his handling of the coronavirus pandemic and that he is behind Joe Biden in election polls. No surprise there. And it should not be a surprise that he fired his campaign manager in another of his shoot-the-messenger moments.

An ABC poll asking people if they were satisfied or not with Trump's handling of the pandemic showed 67 percent unsatisfied and 33 percent satisfied. Better than the previous 55 percent to 45 percent result, but it still beggars belief that a third of the country still think he is handling the crisis well.

President Jair Bolsonaro of Brazil has contracted the virus. He's another disaster, and as Brazil spirals out of control, he does nothing to stop the spread. Unfortunately, his symptoms are minor; and he will recover quickly, allowing him potentially to say, "See, what's the big deal?" I wish he had got a much heavier case as that may have made a difference to his approach. Oh yes, and he's taking hydroxychloroquine—enough said!

Who's a Clever Boy!

Trump seems to give proof that he really did pay someone to sit his SATs—at least the mathematics part. In a 9 July tweet, he is again ranting about testing and writes, "For the 1/100th time, the reason..." There are some great reactions on Twitter to his "1/100th":

> 1/100th is less than one, you idiot. You are an incompetent blowhard, and those aren't even your worst qualities, you idiot. Coronavirus cases are skyrocketing, you idiot. Your mask-less indoor rallies and lack of leadership have helped spread it, you idiot.

> If a kid in the fifth grade wrote this tweet for a paper he would get an F for poor grammar. For the 1/100th time? What the fuck is this guy talking about...

> Let's break this shitshow of a tweet down. 1) 1/100th doesn't mean what you think it means. 2) Other countries are testing more and doing better. 3) Testing fewer people doesn't mean we have fewer cases. Just means we've found fewer cases. 4) You are fucking awful at math.

Abo-u-u-u-t Turn!

21 July: Well, I suppose it had to happen, but why now? At yesterday's coronavirus briefing, the first one in about three months, America's unstable genius performs alone. Dr. Fauci is not invited, and Dr. Birx is reportedly somewhere in the background. But the

good news is that Trump now supports the wearing of masks and, unbelievably, says he wears one regularly.

It's all bollocks, of course, but what has made him rethink his position when states like Florida, California, Arizona, and Texas are spiraling even further out of control? Perhaps he finally realises that the scientists are right. I doubt it. Perhaps it's because more than 142,000 Americans have lost their lives to coronavirus—definitely not. But wait. Perhaps it's because he's tanking in the polls. *Bingo!* That's all he cares about.

So should we be happy that Trump has finally come down in favour of masks? Yes, but we know that's not the position he wants to project to his base. He even acknowledges that things will "get worse before they get better" but blames the spike in cases on younger people attending protests, which may prove true, but he also blames Mexicans coming across the border. Of course he does!

Despite his epiphany on masks, Trump still wants schools to open in the autumn. He ignores any advice against opening and, in a roundabout way, argues a case that children pose less of a risk. He may well be right, but just saying "open the schools" is not a strategy.

The Fat One is determined to push this to the limit because if schools are open in the autumn, just before the election, he can say the country is back on track. It's all about how things look at election time, not how things are.

One final thing, last weekend as new case numbers in Florida were levelling off, some six hundred morons gathered for a block party, which had to be broken up by police—no masks and no social distancing. We now wait for the next two weeks or so to see how many of them have contracted coronavirus.

This is irresponsible beyond belief. They are a bunch of witless wankers. As frustrated as I am, I don't want them to get the virus because if they do, it will just keep spreading. I just want them to be sensible. Is that really too much to ask?

US Hits Four Million COVID-19 Cases

23 July sees four million cases and 144,000 deaths. Heartbreaking. It takes ninety days for the US to reach its first one million cases but only fifteen days to go from three million to four million.

I am fascinated to see that Trump is ignoring the mess in the more southern states as they pay the price for following his urging to open early. Instead, he is claiming credit for successes in the more northerly states, who ignored him.

Trump Sends in the Troops

He's at it again. Nearly two months after the death of George Floyd, protests continue in Portland, Oregon, but Trump has a solution: send in the troops. Well, strictly speaking, they are not troops but police dressed as troops carrying big guns and firing tear gas at people—just how Trump likes it.

To defend his actions, he cites murder rates in New York, Philadelphia, Minneapolis, and Chicago and makes an announcement at a White House press briefing, saying, "Frankly, we have no choice but to get involved. Politicians running many of our cities have put interests of criminals above law-abiding citizens. These same politicians have now embraced the far-left movement to break up our police departments, causing violent crime in their cities to spiral—and I mean spiral seriously—out of control."

However, Mr. Wannabe Dictator's get-tough policy turns out to be a let's-make-things-worse policy as civil unrest in Portland only increases. What doesn't help is that federal agents are accused of taking people away in unmarked cars without any hint of probable cause. As Trump might say, things could get worse before they get better.

"For Me, I Have to Protect the American People"

The 2020 Republican National Convention planned for August, where delegates of the Republican Party select its nominees for president and vice president in the upcoming election, is originally scheduled to be held in Charlotte, North Carolina.

But the Democratic governor, Roy Cooper, insists that it be scaled down due to coronavirus. Naturally, Grumpy Trumpy isn't happy; but the Republican National Committee moves the major celebratory events, including Trump's speech formally accepting the party's nomination, to Jacksonville, Florida.

However, following Trump's mask epiphany, he decides to cancel Florida. What a good chap! Trump tells reporters, with as much sincerity as he can muster, "I looked at my team, and I said the timing for this event is not right. It's just not right with what's happened recently, the flare-up in Florida. To have a big convention, it's not the right time. For me, I have to protect the American people." Sob, sob, pass me the tissues.

And showing his love of "sir" conversations, which are a tell for the fact that he's lying, he goes on to say, "They said, 'Sir, we can make this work very easily.' I said there's nothing more important in our country than keeping our people safe, whether it's from the China virus or the radical-left mob." What a great guy! More tissues, anyone?

Trump Removes Twelve Thousand Troops from Germany

The US has about 34,000 army and air force troops stationed in NATO-ally Germany; but in a surprise move, Trump announces he plans to remove 12,000 of them. The plan is criticised by both Democrats and Republicans, many of whom believe the move will weaken the US military position in Europe and strengthen Russia's. Putin is delighted.

Trump is not doing it for any military or other strategic reason. He tells us on 29 July that he's doing it because Germany is not spending the NATO target of 2 percent of its GDP on defence and because Germany is taking advantage of the US!

Speaking to reporters at the White House, he says, "We spend a lot of money on Germany. They take advantage of us on trade, and they take advantage on the military. So we're reducing the force." In other words, he's a petulant prick and doesn't want to play with them anymore.

But it gets better. About 6,600 troops will return to the US, and the remaining 5,400 are to be moved to Italy and Belgium—another two countries that don't meet the NATO target of spending 2 percent of their GDP on defence! You've just gotta love 'im!

Wait! Hold That Election…

30 July: Back in April, Joe Biden said that Trump would probably come up with a plan to delay the election. He was right. Due to coronavirus, a lot of voting is likely to be done by post, and Trump is suggesting again that voting by mail is liable to significant fraud.

In a tweet this morning, Trump calls for the election to be delayed "until people can properly, securely, and safely vote." Great. Make sure all the schools open but delay the election. OK, the election will not be delayed, but it's a good distraction from people talking about the way he's ballsed up the coronavirus crisis.

August 2020

Yes, Open Those Schools!

This is a subject that rightly deserves everyone's full attention, but it goes without saying that it should be done safely. Trump and his secretary of education, Betsy de Vos, advocate opening all schools without taking into consideration the coronavirus hotspots. Trump does not like the CDC guidelines to opening schools, saying that, among other things, they are "very tough and expensive."

Parents and teachers alike want children back at school, but no one wants the children—and by extension teachers and family members—put at risk. A good example of what not to do is to look at Israel, where they began gradually to open schools in May.

It started well, but what looks like a mix of arrogance and criticism of costs caused the government to take its foot off the brake, resulting in a spike in cases. When schools there began opening in mid-May, new COVID-19 cases were at less than 50 per day. By July, they were around 1,500 a day, thereby undoing all the good work previously done. What a waste! And what a lesson!

This is not rocket science. The more risk we take, the more likely we are to contract the virus. We need to demonstrate that we not only understand how the virus works but also how to adjust our behaviour.

Before they lost the plot, Israel demonstrated that schools can open successfully. It is abundantly clear that a step-by-step approach is the way to go whilst fully recognising there will be an increase in cases.

The prospects of successfully emerging from this shit-show anytime within the next twelve months—absent intelligent school authorities and a good vaccine—don't look good. If authorities recklessly pursue school opening, case numbers will rise; and very possibly, parts of the economy will close again.

We can only hope that as new case numbers and deaths continue to march forward (4.75 million cases and 156,000 deaths as of 4 August) in the face of schools opening, common sense will prevail, and masks and social distancing become the norm.

Failing all, we still have the parents. How many will send their children to school?

What Happened at That Block Party in Florida?

Well, at the time of the party (18 July) reported cases in Florida were 335,000; and today (5 August) eighteen days later, that number is up by 50 percent at 497,000. However, it is not possible to make a direct link with the block party as there is an abundance of other Floridians who have been dining at the table of stupidity.

But there is still some good news to be found; and that is, despite the rise in case numbers, the rate of increase is declining. So at least the daily numbers are going in the right direction once again.

Sadly, the same can't be said for deaths, where the numbers have seen a big spike. Looking at the number of deaths through the seven-day average, we see that exactly one month ago the average daily number was 44. Today it is 185.

Arizona Shows Signs of Improvement

Since mid-June when Arizona's governor Doug Ducey yielded to pressure to retract his statewide ban on local mask requirements and in early July with COVID cases spiking and when he was forced to reverse many of the mid-May openings, there has been a marked improvement in Arizona's fortunes.

What a surprise! In many parts of the state, after local authorities were finally allowed to impose mask-wearing and social distancing requirements, cases went down. It's that simple! With a positivity rate of 12.5 percent, Arizona still has a way to go, but it's heading in the right direction.

But in Texas

The positivity rate has jumped from 4 percent in May to 20 percent today, 11 August, but Texas has cut back on the number of tests being conducted from a high of about seventy-five thousand per day a few weeks ago to forty-five thousand. Although it's not clear why.

More than likely, Governor Greg Abbott doesn't like the results. However, what it does highlight is how COVID has become so politicised with Democratic-run counties within the state generally faring much better than Republican-run counties. Hard to believe these people are adults!

Some Trumpballs: A Reason to Smile—Or Cry

Last week, when visiting a Whirlpool production facility in Ohio, Trump revealed his detailed knowledge of world geography by referring to Thailand as "*Thigh*land."

This reminds me of September 2017, when he hosted a lunch for African leaders. In his opening welcome remarks, Trump referred to Namibia as "Nambia"—he did it twice! Imagine, you're about to host a lunch for leaders of African countries, and you don't even bother to familiarise yourself with the names of the countries they represent. Why would he care? He thinks most of them are "shithole" countries, anyway.

But his latest Trumpballs gaffes came on Monday (10 August) when at a Shite House press briefing, he was talking about the "great pandemic of 1917," referring to the pandemic of 1918, which ended in 1920, taking an estimated fifty million lives worldwide.

Needless to say, fifty million wasn't enough for Trump, so he added a few more for good measure, referring to "anywhere from fifty to one hundred million" lives lost. However, the best part was when he said that the pandemic "probably ended the Second World War." Second? Duh!

I have to say. I will miss him when he's gone, but that said, I can't wait to miss him!

Biden Chooses Kamala Harris as Running Mate

First, a little background: Harris, born in 1964 in California, is the daughter of a Jamaican-born father, who became professor of economics at Harvard University, and an Indian-born mother, who was known for her work on breast cancer. Her parents were divorced when she was six, and she and her younger sister were brought up mostly by their mother.

Harris has a background in law. Rising through the ranks, she became district attorney of San Francisco in 2003 and, seven years later, was voted attorney general of California, winning reelection in 2014. In 2016, she won election to the US Senate. She ran for the 2020 Democratic presidential nomination and did well at the beginning but could not maintain her momentum, ultimately ending her campaign in December 2019.

And now, here she is as Joe Biden's running mate for the 2020 presidential election! The press are keen to report that on 11 August 2020, she became the first African American and the first Asian American to be chosen as the running mate of a major party's presidential candidate. I hope she can continue to add to her list of firsts, especially in November!

Biden said long ago that he would choose a female running mate, and Harris was one of a number of candidates. Biden was spoilt for choice, but Harris looks like a good one. She has proven herself a tough interrogator in the Senate. She's intelligent. She can think on her feet and comes across as being credible.

She is likely to do well in debates with VP Pence. My only concern at this very early stage is that she is not particularly charismatic, but I hope by being punched about a bit in the coming eighty days before the election, she will find her stride.

Trump clearly has some concerns as despite her appointment being less than two days old, he is already taking a few jabs, describing her as mean, nasty, and angry; and saying she's "sort of a madwoman." And best of all, he is joining a suggestion that she may not really be an American. Familiar? He is such a charmer, this lard-arsed leader.

It's Convention Time!

Conventions are mostly of interest only to those who attend. The party leaders each lay out the best way forward, with the incumbent party saying what a great job it's done and the opposition saying the opposite. They nominate their respective leaders, who accept their respective nominations.

First to go was the Democrats whose four day conference began on 17 August. They pull out all the big guns, including Hillary and Bill Clinton, Michelle and Barack Obama, and many more. They all say good things about Biden and bad things about Trump. They say how the world is a worse place because of Trump and how it will be a better place with Biden as president.

The Republicans' four-day bash begins on 24 August and is broadly similar, apart from being a total Trump-praising exercise with seemingly every member of his family giving speeches saying how wonderful he is and how the world is a better place because of him and how it will become a terrible place if Biden became president. All good familiar stuff.

A Brief Trip to the UK

Our son, Sebastian, who is at university in London, came to New York in November 2019 to spend Christmas and New Year with us. His intention was to return to the UK in early January and find an internship for the remainder of his holiday.

But coronavirus put paid to those plans, and instead, he ended up spending the next ten months with us here in New York. And as luck would have it, he found an internship in New York, although after only a short period was forced to work from home.

What an irony it is that this pandemic gave us ten months with our son, which otherwise we would never have had.

There was however something very odd about those times. He and I would spend evenings baking lemon drizzle cake and more besides, but we had to stop as I realised that all that baking was causing the clothes in my wardrobe to shrink! How weird is that?

So here we are in London, helping Sebastian settle into his newly rented flat prior to resuming his studies. Being here means I am mercifully spared the second-by-second account of convention events in the US where the real fun will start in a few weeks when the debates get underway.

London is quite a contrast to New York when it comes to mask-wearing. In New York, I would estimate that 85 percent of people wear masks outside, whereas in London, I would put that figure no higher than 30 percent. It therefore comes as no surprise that coronavirus cases have seen a large spike in the UK, prompting Prime Minister Boris Johnson to introduce the "rule of six," meaning no more than six people can gather together indoors.

There are variations of this rule in Wales, Scotland, and Northern Ireland, thus ensuring no one has even the remotest idea of what they can do.

September 2020

It's Rally Time Again

I'm back in New York, in time to see Fanta-Man, oblivious to anything but his own desires, going ahead with an indoor rally in Henderson (near Las Vegas), Nevada. Unlike the poorly attended Tulsa rally in May, this time, the crowds look much larger. But Trump's team does not release any numbers, nor can I find any other indication of crowd size.

Mask-wearing at the rally is encouraged; but very few are worn, with the exception of those who are behind Trump at the podium, for whom mask-wearing is compulsory.

Given the sheer number of those not wearing masks, Trump's rally looks like another breeding ground for spreading the virus. Interesting that it took place against the backdrop of cases in the US exceeding 6.5 million and deaths nearing 195,000—neither of which gets a mention. But, hey, the markets are up!

We see what has happened in other countries. As people lower their guard, case numbers rise. The prospect here, therefore, can only be in for more heartache in the months ahead. We are already seeing examples dotted about the country where students are holding parties with no regard for the potential consequences of their actions. Even allowing for COVID fatigue, this is still reckless behaviour.

There is no doubt that maintaining one's resolve to contain COVID-19 is difficult. In the beginning, it was easier. We were nervous because we could see the numbers of infections and deaths climbing every day with no end in sight.

However, now that a number of states have "managed the curve," it is much more difficult to remain focused. The transgressors appear mostly to be students and millennials.

Trump Promotes Herd "Mentality"

More Trumpballs! In an ABC town hall-style interview on 15 September, Trump again demonstrates his full grasp of the English language and of all matters medical by promoting herd "mentality" as the way forward. Genius!

OK, he means herd immunity, where a virus is allowed to spread on its own and enough people become infected and develop antibodies such that its further spread is drastically reduced. Nice idea. And it can work, but that is normally only after vaccines are in place.

Fauci said a week ago that given the extent of obesity, hypertension, and diabetes in the US, the death toll through following the herd immunity route would be "enormous and totally unacceptable." Note: Research done by the Harvard T.H. Chan School of Public Health estimates that as of 2019, around 40 percent of Americans are considered obese and 18 percent are considered severely obese.

Another Book on Trump

15 September: Since Dodgy Don took office, there have been more than 1,200 books written about him! One of the latest is written by Bob Woodward, a journalist who, together with Carl Bernstein, became famous for their investigation into the Watergate scandal in 1972 and their subsequent book *All the President's Men*, which was later made into a film.

Woodward's new book, *Rage*, is based on eighteen approved recordings of interviews with Trump between December 2019 and July 2020.

It is notable for the fact that in February, Trump understood exactly how dangerous COVID-19 was and admitted to deliberately playing it down to avoid panicking people.

Don't forget, on 26 February, he said cases in the US would soon be "close to zero" and a day later he said, "It will disappear—it's like a miracle."

On a call on 14 August, Woodward tells Trump that his book is "tough" and "close to the bone."

And Trump's response? "You know the market's coming back very strong. You do know that."

Trump, totally ignoring coronavirus, repeatedly asks Woodward if he intends to portray him positively in the book. This alone is proof of his incompetence in running a country. He shouldn't even be allowed to run a bath.

CDC Boss "Mistaken" and "Confused"

16 September: In a jaw-dropping press briefing, Trump says CDC boss Robert Redfield was "mistaken" and "confused" when he gave evidence to Congress that in his opinion, a coronavirus vaccine wouldn't be widely available until midway through 2021.

Trump also went for Redfield after he said, "This face mask is more guaranteed to protect me against COVID than when I take a COVID vaccine. If I don't get an immune response, the vaccine's not going to protect me. This face mask will."

Trump says Redfield has "misunderstood" the question. He didn't. No vaccine is 100 percent effective, so if it doesn't work on you, the mask will continue to give you protection. Needless to say, we will later discover that not only are vaccines developed in record time, they also have an almost unprecedented efficacy rate of over 90 percent.

I close this section with one final gem from the briefing. Of course, the Pink Porker has done a fabulous job, and the death toll would have been much higher if he hadn't taken all the mitigation measures. But the gem is his criticism of states governed by Democrats, the so-called "blue states."

"Blue" in the United States represents the left political spectrum, and "red" represents the right. It is the opposite in the United Kingdom. However, while their policies may be similar in some respects, they cannot be compared.

He says, "The blue states had tremendous death rates. If you take the blue states out, we're at a level that I don't think anybody in the world would be at. We're really at a very low level." Whaaaat?

Social media was full of comments, saying the US is still near the top of the world's worst death toll list even with the blue states removed from the equation. But, hey, it's not the truth that matters. It's getting the statement out there.

The "Notorious RBG"—15 March 1933–18 September 2020

Ruth Bader Ginsburg—a Brooklyn-born justice on the Supreme Court, where she served for twenty-seven years—dies, aged eighty-seven, on 18 September of complications of metastatic pancreatic cancer. The Senate vote approving her as a justice in 1993 was ninety-six to three—one senator was at a funeral. You don't see votes like that today.

She was a tiny woman, just about five feet tall and weighing no more than one hundred pounds soaking wet; but she was as tough, as strong, and as determined as they come, overcoming five bouts of cancer and numerous operations. She was a trailblazer for women's rights and, as importantly, for equal rights; and that meant fighting for men, as well as women.

Her nickname was given to her in 2013 by a then law student, Shana Knizhnik, as a result of reading some of the fiery opinions she had written as a justice of the Supreme Court. The name was a play on "The Notorious BIG," a famous fellow Brooklyn-born rapper. Ginsburg loved the name and enjoyed the celebrity that came with it.

Her achievements are countless, but one particular case early in her career deserves a mention. In 1975, she appealed a case to the Supreme Court of a man who argued he was entitled to Social Security survivor benefits. His wife, the family breadwinner, had died in childbirth. But the Social Security Act of 1935 held that men were assumed to be the breadwinners, so survivor benefits were only payable to widows, not widowers.

Ginsburg argued and won the case with eight of the nine justices finding for her client. They concluded the 1935 act was unconstitutional on the basis of gender bias,[7] and she just carried on from there!

Her legacy is enormous. She was the architect of so much change, and it is no exaggeration to say that the lives of every woman—and man for that matter—in America today are better thanks to her relentless fight for equal rights.

There is so much more that can be said about RBG, but the sadness of her death only weeks before an election is not the story. The story is about what is happening because of it.

Already, Democrats and Republicans are arguing whether she should be replaced on the Supreme Court now or after the next election. The poor woman hasn't been dead twenty-four hours, and the fighting has already started.

Don't You Just Love Politicians?

In 2016, when Obama was president, Justice Antonin Scalia died unexpectedly nine months before the election. Republicans then, as now, controlled the Senate; and Mitch McConnell, Senate majority leader, used the power of his office to refuse holding a hearing for Obama's nominee, saying, "The American people should have a voice in the selection of their next Supreme Court justice. Therefore, this vacancy should not be filled until we have a new president."

So no hearing, no replacement. But only two weeks after Trump takes office in February, a new Republican justice, Neil Gorsuch, is appointed.

---

[7] This case came after a number of similar cases where gender bias was unsuccessfully argued (not by Ginsburg), making her victory all the more impressive.

Now in a similar situation, following RBG's death only weeks before the election, Mitchell argues the opposite, saying we should *not* wait for a new president to be elected! We can all scream "hypocrisy," but the Democrats would have done exactly the same thing.

So what does that tell us? Actually, it tells us nothing we don't already know. Almost all politicians are self-serving, working only for their own advancement and power.

They will tell you what they think you want to hear and promise to deliver to you on your every wish. But what do they actually do? They do whatever will advance them personally and whatever they are told to do by those who have funded their election.

They have no honour and no morals. They are the personification of disingenuousness and do not give a stuff about the voters, at least not until elections loom again.

When America lost Senator John McCain to brain cancer in 2018, it lost a principled, honest, and genuine man. He was one of an endangered species—a politician of integrity.

Back in October 2008 when he was the Republican presidential candidate, he defended Obama against a woman in a town hall audience, who made disparaging remarks about him, saying she had read that he was "an Arab." McCain stepped in by saying, "No, ma'am, he's a decent family man that I just happen to have disagreements with on fundamental issues, and that is what this campaign is all about."

At that same gathering, McCain had earlier defended Obama against another critic who suggested he was linked with domestic terrorists. Again, McCain interrupted, saying, "No, he is a person you do not have to be scared of as president of the United States."

Those were the days. Will the next John McCain please step forward!

And while we wait, we will watch the combatants. Trump has already said he will go ahead with a Supreme Court justice nomination and that it will be a woman. She will have to appear before the Senate Judiciary Committee, which is a mouth-water-ing prospect as one of the committee members is none other than Joe Biden's own prospective VP, Kamala Harris!

Despite Harris's reputation as a tough questioner, it will mean nothing if she performs badly. The stakes are high for her. Trump will go after Harris whether she does well or badly, but if badly, he will rip her to shreds. I cannot imagine that in her wildest dreams, Harris ever considered this as a possibility.

Sorry, but I Have to Mention Senator Lindsey Graham

My apologies for what may seem an unrelated diversion, but bear with me. However, before I start, I need to tell you my position: Lindsey Graham is an arse.

Graham was a longtime friend and colleague of Senator John McCain, upon whose death tweeted, "America and Freedom have lost one of her greatest champions…and I've lost one of my dearest friends and mentor."

However, all was not quite how it seemed. Being a friend of McCain gave him visibility. He had grabbed onto McCain's coattails and got a free ride to greater recognition and respect. When McCain died, Graham's behaviour changed, and he started sucking up to Trump.

Along with almost all other Republican senators, Graham declares he is in favour of appointing a new justice ahead of the upcoming election to replace RBG. No surprise there, given Republicans control the Senate. However, this position is the polar opposite to that which he so eloquently expressed in 2016 following the death of Justice Scalia.

Back then, he was strongly *opposed* to voting in a new justice, saying at a Senate hearing, "I want you to use my words against me. If there's a Republican president in 2016 and a vacancy occurs in the last year of the first term, you can say Lindsey Graham said, 'Let's let the next president, whoever it might be, make that nomination.'"

He argued that if Republicans changed the rules, they would be guilty of "abuse of power." He said there would be "no more reaching across the aisle" where parties seek each other's views on suitable candidates but instead would "pick the most hard-assed people we can find."

He was right; but for context, the leading candidates seeking to become the next Republican president were then Tosser Ted Cruz and Fat Boy Trump, both of whom Graham disliked at the time.

A quick note on Cruz: Trump accused Cruz's father of being connected with the assassination of John F. Kennedy. Obviously, this was crap, but Trump was happy just to sow the seed of doubt. Trump subsequently attacked Cruz and his family whenever he had the chance. Cruz's response was to say, "I am not in the habit of supporting people who attack my wife and attack my father."

Utter bullshit as later he was kissing Trump's arse, together with every other disingenuous politician who thought Trump could help them. What a pathetic plonker Cruz is! It's ironic that when campaigning for the presidency in 2016, Trump gave Cruz the nickname of "Lying Ted"! I think that may have been the last time Trump told the truth.

Anyway, back to Loser Lindsey as I want to say, "Thank you, Lindsey," for asking us to use your words against you. We do! Looking back, it is obvious you were lying, not just because we could hear your voice or see your lips moving. It's just what you do.

Your truth is whatever is right for you in the moment. Like Cruz, you are devoid of moral fibre. It is a blessing you are not married with children. I cannot imagine what life any child of yours would have, having to explain you away.

Lindsey, me ole' mate, it's great that you've become a regular supporter and golf partner of Burger Boy, so maybe that explains why you flip-flopped on the matter of electing a new justice.

But wait. You've flip-flopped before. When McDonald was a mere candidate rolling out his borrowed Make America Great Again[8] slogan, you weren't such a fan then, were you? No. In fact,

---

[8] The slogan "Make America Great Again" was originally used by Ronald Reagan during his 1980 election campaign.

in December 2015, you told CNN, "You know how you make America great again? Tell Donald Trump to go to hell." And for good measure, you described Obese-Wan Kenobi as a "race-baiting, xenophobic, religious bigot." Great stuff, Lindsey.

May the false be with you!

22 September 2020: Two Hundred Thousand Lives Lost

According to Johns Hopkins University, the death toll in America is 200,000 out of a worldwide total of 970,000. Total cases in the US are just short of 6.9 million with 31.4 million worldwide. These numbers, by any standard of measurement, are terrible.

Other monitoring agencies show the US reached the 200,000 milestone a week ago, but no matter. It gives us another moment when we should reflect on exactly what's going on around us and ask ourselves, "Are we doing enough? Can we do more? Are the country's leaders doing the right things?"

Well, according to Trump, the answer to all the questions is an unequivocal "Yes!" He was asked a couple of days ago how he would rate his handling of the pandemic. His answer? "I'd give myself an A+."

Agreed, if A is for arsehole.

If I Lose, I'll Snooze—In the Oval Office

Concerns increase as to whether Trump will go quietly if he loses the November election. On Wednesday, he is asked if he will commit to a peaceful transfer of power, but he does not answer the question directly.

Instead, his response is to say, "Well, we're going to have to see what happens. You know that." He then shifts to one of his manufactured pet hates and says, "I've been complaining very strongly about the ballots, and the ballots are a disaster."

Trump has been bleating about mail-in ballots for months, complaining they are riddled with fraud, but so far, neither he nor his campaign has offered any supporting evidence—because there is none! His strategy is simple: if he loses, he will blame voter fraud and will do whatever he can to hold on to office.

On Thursday, 24 September, he agrees in a Fox interview with a comment made by Loser Lindsey to abide by any decision made by the Supreme Court on who the winner is, should it ever come to that. Supreme Court? No wonder he's so desperate to get a new justice before the election.

Senator Angus King (Independent) from Maine makes the observation, as do many others, that more Democrats are likely to vote by mail than Republicans, who will prefer in-person voting. This means that as in-person votes are counted more quickly, the early results may well favour Trump, but then move in favour Biden as the mail-in votes are counted.

Should that be the case, Trump will definitely declare fraud. I can almost hear him giving a "what did I tell you?" speech. Cue the Supreme Court!

So the prospects for a smooth handover, if there is one, are small. The only thing that may keep Trump quiet is if Biden wins by a landslide, but even then he will doubtlessly scream that fraud was on a massive scale.

Thanks to Trump, another concern that has not been aired much so far is the prospect of protests, or worse, whoever wins—especially if the margin of victory is small. The best solution would be for Democrats to do in-person voting and for Biden to have a landslide victory![9]

28 September 2020—Another Sad Day

Only recently I noted that COVID deaths in the US had reached two hundred thousand, but less than a week later, cases have broken through the seven-million barrier. Today also tragi-

---

[9] Although it was abundantly clear Trump would not lose with grace, I had no idea, when writing this part, what lay ahead.

cally marks the day when deaths worldwide passed one million as worldwide cases pushed thirty-four million.

Trump Is Looking "Taxed"

Well done to *The New York Times* for publishing a story exposing Trump as a total fraud. "But that's not news!" I hear you cry. No, it's not, but it may just be the beginning of ever-Trumpers realising that they should rethink their position. I very much doubt it, but I live in hope!

In what is described variously as "bombshell" and "explosive," a *NYT* article begins with "*The Times* obtained Donald Trump's tax information extending over more than two decades, revealing struggling properties, vast write-offs, an audit battle, and hundreds of millions in debt coming due."

Trump's response to the revelations is straight from his playbook, telling reporters, "It's fake news, totally fake news. Made up. Fake. The IRS does not treat me well. They treat me like the Tea Party. They don't treat me well. They treat me very badly. You have people in the IRS. They treat me very, very badly…" Well, that was clear!

Donny also vents out on Twitter, saying the article is fake and, today, 28 September, says *The NYT* got the information illegally. Well, which one is it, Don? Fake or illegally obtained?

We learn from *The NYT* that between 2000 and 2015, Trump paid federal taxes in only five of those years. But to be fair, the toxic tosser did pay taxes in 2016 and 2017—$750 in each year. Yes, $750! WTF?

We also learn that Dodgy Don is deep in debt and that loans totaling more than $420 million, for which he is personally responsible, fall due over the next four years. It is not clear who the creditors are or where they are, but questions of national security are being raised should the lenders be able to leverage their position.

We are told that $100 million of that debt was taken out on Trump Tower in New York and is due for repayment in 2022. A further $125 million is owed by the Doral Golf Club in Miami and $160 million by the Washington Hotel. To add to his woes, he may be forced to repay a $72.9 million income-tax refund received in 2010, which, with interest and possible penalties, could amount to $100 million.

The article says his golf courses and hotels have been losing money for years and that he has been propping up his businesses from money he made from *The Apprentice*, which he hosted for fourteen seasons.

That money has apparently run out; so with high expenses and reduced income, combined with his track record of being bankrupt four times already, it is hard to see where he'll get the money from to meet his obligations.

He has spent his entire life overtrading and has spectacularly demonstrated zero business acumen. *NYT* put it best when they wrote, "Ultimately, Mr. Trump has been more successful playing a business mogul than being one in real life."

NYT has taken a leaf out of Dodgy Don's book and promised more to come, but let's round off with a couple of goodies. Trump claimed a $70,000 deduction for hairstyling during his time on *The Apprentice* and, through the Trump Corporation, paid his daughter some $740,000 in consulting fees, which may have been OK if she wasn't already an employee of the Trump Corporation! Paying consulting fees to an employee?

29 September—The First Trump-Biden Presidential Debate

In what many are describing as a "shambles" and a "chaotic ninety minutes," Trump shows himself to be ignorant, arrogant, and a man in fear of losing the election. The debate is moderated by Chris Wallace of Fox News. Wallace turns out to be a good choice but is given a rough ride.

He is fair to both candidates but struggles to control Trump, who repeatedly interrupts proceedings—something both sides had agreed not to do. Had somebody from CNN or CNBC been moderating, they would doubtlessly have been accused of going after

Trump, but Wallace correctly admonishes him like a schoolboy—several times.

Biden, on the other hand, fares pretty well. I was concerned how he would perform because we have seen in the past that when he gets flustered, he speaks far too quickly and can lose his train of thought.

This time, he keeps it together and is calm, although on one occasion, he does tell the orange person next to him to "shut up, man." Oh yes, he also calls him a clown, a racist, and the worst president America has ever had. But apart from that…

In truth, there is nothing memorable in the debate, but Trump yet again refuses to denounce White supremacists. Wallace asks, "Are you willing tonight to condemn White supremacists and militia groups and to say that they need to stand down?"

Trump replies, "Proud Boys,[10] stand back and stand by! But I'll tell you what. Somebody's got to do something about antifa and the left."

End of round 1—advantage Biden.

---

[10] The Anti-Defamation League describes the Proud Boys as a hate group that uses violence to advance an ideological agenda. It calls it "misogynistic, Islamophobic, transphobic, anti-immigration," as well as "White supremacist and anti-Semitic."

October 2020

Trump Gets the Virus

2 October: He's positive—for coronavirus—as is his wife. It couldn't have happened to a more deserving man. His cavalier approach and his dreadful management of the pandemic make it no surprise he got it. Am I sorry? Absolutely not, but I don't wish him harm.

Despite his age and being fat and orange, recovery statistics are in his favour, and although I hope he recovers, I also hope his road to recovery is bumpy and teaches him to stop being such a prat. I doubt it will, but again, I live in hope.

One scenario I dread, however, is of Trump getting only a mild dose. Should that be the case, I can see him becoming even more insufferable.

I didn't mention it earlier; but during the debate, Trump was scornful of Biden wearing a mask, saying, "Every time you see him, he's wearing a mask," and says that he, Trump, only wears one when he needs to. Trump is essentially saying that Biden wears a mask for show, but he wears one only when there is a need to. Looks like Trumpty Dumpty missed out on one of those need-to-wear moments!

I make no pretense of being sympathetic to Trump's woes and would have even less sympathy for his family, if they were to follow Dumpy Daddy on the path to infection.

In their arrogance, they removed their masks just before the debate with Biden began and, in a childish act of defiance, refused to put them back on when asked to do so by one of the doctors at the venue. What a bunch of lowlife grandstanders!

In the evening, Trump is taken to the Walter Reed Medical Center out of "an abundance of caution," but no substantive information has been given as to his state of health. He will stay there for "a number of days" but is not thought to be in a serious condition. How reassuring to see Trump shifting from an absence of caution to an abundance!

3 October: Between yesterday and today, a whole bunch of White House staff and three Republican senators test positive, but this comes as no surprise as Trump has recently been holding rallies all over the place.

Perhaps the major source of infection is from a bash held in the Rose Garden last week where Trump announced Amy Barrett, a far-right, devoutly religious individual, as his proposed candidate for the newly vacant Supreme Court justice slot. At that event, people were seated without any distancing and 99 percent of them without masks. After displays like that, you reap what you sow.

To update the nation, a bunch of Trump's doctors gather outside the hospital to talk about his state of health, but it's a fairly meaningless exercise. They either avoid answering or evade reporters' questions and later are heavily criticised for it.

But the next day, my worst fears come true—he is recovering quickly. In fact, he's feeling so much better that he arranges to be given a drive around the hospital so he can wave to his fans and infect those in the car with him. His doctor says Trump will likely be released tomorrow to continue his recovery at the White House.

Reports from "sources close to the president" are saying that it is Trump himself who insists he gets out of hospital because he does not want to appear weak. Meanwhile, more White House staff contract the virus, including Press Secretary Kayleigh McEnany and two of her staff.

Prior to returning to the White House, Trump tweets, "Don't be afraid of COVID. Don't let it dominate your life." Tell that to the families of the 210,000 Americans who have died so far. What a dick!

Trump's arrival at the White House is pure comedic farce. In the early evening filled with a cocktail of drugs, he returns to the White House, walks up the steps while struggling for breath, and poses Mussolini-like on the terrace without a mask, saluting his departing helicopter. He then goes inside, only to come out again with a film crew so he can repeat the whole tin-pot dictator performance again for a campaign video.

He really does not see the world laughing at him. This is a pathetic, ego-driven performance by someone who has no idea what to do. All the medical experts are dismayed by his mask-less performance, and as usual, the spreader-in-chief doesn't give a shit. Situation normal!

Update on COVID

Things are not measurably improving, and the prospect of any significant improvement in the future appears small, especially as we approach the winter months. Total US cases are 7.5 million and deaths, 210,000.

The numbers are plateauing at 700-plus deaths a day and 42,000 daily cases, which is not good. Cases in half the states are beginning to tick up, and in some states, so are hospitalisations.

Even More Coronavirus Cases at the White House!

If it wasn't so pathetic, it would be funny. Today, 7 October 2020, we learn that there are now twenty people, either recent visitors to or workers at the White House, who have contracted the virus. A great example of leadership at its best!

But wait! It's not all bad news. Among those infected is the loathsome Stephen Miller. Miller is a far-right, anti-immigration, promoter of White nationalist publications, conspiracy theorist, and total shit.

Oh yes, and he's Chubby Chump's senior advisor on immigration policy! Whilst I wish him a long and unpleasant recovery, I wonder if any of the people treating him will be from India, China, or any other country from where the US accepts immigrants. I do hope so!

The Pence-Harris Debate

Last night saw the only debate between Mike Pence and Kamala Harris. Despite all the pre-debate interest, it turned out to be a bit of a nonevent. There were no fireworks, no shouting, and no memorable moments.

One thing that did stick out was Pence regularly exceeding his allotted time to answer questions, which looked like a deliberate tactic to irritate and frustrate Kamala Harris. Unlike me, Harris did not react, despite my shouting at the television. Instead, she smiled and asked for equal time from the moderator—which she got.

The post-debate consensus was that Kamala Harris's job for the evening was not to lose Biden's lead in the polls. If that was the objective, then it was job done. But it didn't do much to promote her as being someone who could step into the president's shoes if or when needed.

Trump Boxes Himself into a Corner

We know from Bob Woodward's book, *Rage*, that Trump knew of the seriousness of coronavirus back in February but hid it from the American public and decided to do nothing. He's been found out and now has nowhere to hide.

His problems are compounded because having recovered from coronavirus, Trump's ego prevents him from saying, "OK, we have a problem. I have spoken with the health experts, and here's what we're going to do." Instead, he sticks with "It will all go away. It will disappear." More Trump shit.

But he's boxed himself into a corner, so what does he do? He holds a series of rallies, and Trump fans are lapping it up even as case numbers are increasing all over the country. Today, 13 October, daily cases are averaging fifty-one thousand, up from forty-two thousand only a week ago.

Daily deaths are still in the low seven hundreds, but given the increase in cases, those numbers too are likely to rise. However, improvements in treatment methods mean death rates are not as high, but even so, hospitalization numbers are on the rise.

Is Trump Throwing a "Hail Mary" to Win a Second Term?

What is Trump's strategy? Despite cases being on the up, he is holding one rally after another, putting more people at risk; but why? Maybe because he's behind in the polls, he feels the need to do something drastic, so why not go for all or nothing?

When Trump won in 2016, he gained a lot of support from suburban women, who were crucial in helping him to victory. However, recent polling suggests that these voters are moving toward Biden.

At a rally in Johnstown, Pennsylvania, a key state for both, he gives some indication that he may indeed be concerned about the polls when he pleads, "Suburban women, will you please like me?"

He doesn't care about new coronavirus cases and deflects any criticism by citing the rise in European countries. He talks about "the vaccines," "the therapeutics," and "the cure," all of which are "coming very soon." As far as we know, they're not—at least we didn't know then!

As always, the facts don't matter, but the message does. And he does all he can to convince people that he should be the one to run the country, not those socialists and Marxists.

Rallies, therefore, look like the way to go. After all, they worked last time—and to hell with the virus. If he wins, whatever the coronavirus numbers may be, it won't matter because he's got his second term, and that's all he's ever wanted.

He will be free to continue monetising his position and further divide the country. If he loses, then Biden will inherit one huge mess, and Trump will criticise him at every turn. He'll probably even suggest that Dipshit Jr. run for president or, even worse, his Barbie doll daughter!

Can We Believe the Polls?

Yes! And no! Currently, polls have Biden ahead with an eleven-point lead: fifty-two to forty-one. Pretty convincing, right? Wrong, because this is a national poll, which means far less. Don't forget that Hillary Clinton was well ahead in the 2016 national polls, and she won the popular vote by 2.8 million. But she still lost the election.

This can happen because of the structure of the Electoral College. The Electoral College today has 538 electors, comprising 100 senators, 435 members of the House of Representatives and three electors from the District of Colombia, (better known as Washington DC), which is not a state.

It is formed every four years to perform the ceremonial act of voting into office a president and a vice president. To win an election, a simple majority of 270 electoral votes is required.

People argue, even today, about the reasons Hillary lost to Trump, but the peculiarities of the Electoral College certainly played a role. With the exceptions of Maine (4 votes) and Nebraska (5 votes), the winner of the popular vote in a state is awarded all the Electoral College votes of that state.

The seemingly random number of 435 state representatives was finally decided in 1929 as it was considered to be a "manageable number of members." Previously, the number had been growing in line with the population in each state and therefore needed to be capped.

Today, the number of representatives each state receives from the 435 depends on its proportion of the population as determined by a census that is carried out every ten years. For example, in 1990,

Texas had thirty representatives but, because of the growth in its population relative to the rest of the country, today has thirty-eight.

This allows a candidate to win a closely contested state election by the narrowest of margins but still garner all that state's college votes. And that's exactly what befell Hillary in three of these so-called swing states in 2016—and here lies the twist.

Clinton lost the popular state votes in Wisconsin by 0.7 percent, Michigan by 0.3 percent, and Pennsylvania by 0.7 percent. Together, these states, which represent less than 10 percent of the country's population, delivered 46 electoral votes[11] to Trump; and so he won the election by 306 to 232 votes. Had Hillary won those states, it would instead have given her a victory of 278 to 240. Small margin wins can have huge consequences.

That's rather a long-winded way of explaining one of the foibles of the Electoral College system, but it shows why national polls can be misleading, or even meaningless. Trump may well be behind in the national polls, but he still has everything to fight for. And he knows it.

For Biden, those same states are in play today; and Trump is throwing everything he has at them, as well as Florida (29 votes), another one in the balance. He fully understands that victory in these states—even by the smallest of margins—can pay big dividends. Both Trump and Biden know this is not so much a national election but a state-by-state election. So its game on! What a crazy system.

Also, let's not forget Trump's habit of pulling something out the bag at the last minute to distract voters or discredit his opponent. I'm sure he'll try to do the same again. Maybe *The New York Times* will be able to counter any such move with more revelations about his taxes!

Dr Fauci Is "a Disaster"

On Sunday, 18 October, Fauci appears on *60 Minutes* and, in a wide-ranging interview, is asked if he is surprised that Trump

---

[11] Wisconsin, 10 votes; Michigan, 16; and Pennsylvania, 20.

contracted COVID. He replies that seeing the Rose Garden event a couple of weeks ago on television and seeing so many people packed closely together without masks, he is not surprised that Trump catches the virus nor that it turns into a super-spreader event.

Fauci is also asked for his reaction to a recent election campaign advert in which comments he made several months ago were taken out of context, portraying his support for Trump. He is not a happy chappy. He says he has never publicly endorsed any candidate and is "really ticked off" that he has been misrepresented.

Trump is upset by Fauci's comments and says on a call to campaign workers the following morning, "Fauci is a disaster. People are tired of coronavirus. People are tired of hearing Fauci and all these idiots."

Absolutely brilliant! First Trump tries to jump on Fauci's bandwagon of popularity and, when that fails, says he's an idiot.

Trump has this belief that no one knows better than him, so whatever he does is right. But at the moment, he looks out of control. He continues to insist the corner has been turned on coronavirus when the reality is that cases are rising at an alarming rate across the country.

The only place Trump looks happy is at his key-state rallies, which he continues to hold one after another—even two and sometimes three a day on occasion. Biden, on the other hand, is relatively quiet at the moment, which does not seem like the cleverest move. But there are still two weeks to go, and a lot can happen in that time.

Maybe he's preparing for the debate with Trump later this week.

On Your Marks, Get Set, GObama!

On the eve of the final debate, former president Barack Obama gives a thirty-five-minute speech in Philadelphia, Pennsylvania, and what a speech it is! Seeing and hearing Obama again reminds us what a great speaker he is. When he has spoken previously about this presidency, he rarely, if ever, mentioned Trump by name; but it's always been clear who he's talking about.

This time it's different, and he goes after Trump big time! He says, "I never thought Donald Trump would embrace my vision or continue my policies, but I did hope for the sake of the country that he might show some interest in taking the job seriously."

Obama shows how weak and ineffective a president Trump is, saying, "This president wants full credit for the economy he inherited and no blame for the pandemic he ignored." He adds, "Tweeting at the television doesn't fix things!" His speech is filled with attacks on Trump and praise for Biden and Harris.

In a lighter moment, reminding us of Trump's attacks on Biden's son for his activities in China, Obama cites reports that Trump continues to do business with China and notes he has just been discovered to have "a secret Chinese bank account,"[12] whoops! "How is that possible?" he asks.

He jokes that if he'd had a secret Chinese account while running for reelection, Fox News might have been a little concerned about that, saying, "They would have called me Beijing Barry." Fox News has so far not reported on this discovery.

Obama directs part of his closing remarks to young voters and to the Black community. He urges people to ignore the polls and to go out and vote, stressing, "What we do these next thirteen days will matter for decades to come."

Referring to the last election, he adds, "We've got to turn out like never before. We cannot leave any doubt in this election. We can't be complacent. I don't care about the polls. There were a whole bunch of polls last time, [it] didn't work out because a whole bunch of people stayed at home and got lazy and complacent. Not this time."

Obama has set things up nicely for the debate as Trump will likely be angered by what was said about him. However, the rules

---

[12] Trump's "secret" bank account in China was just reported by *The New York Times*. *The NYT* also noted that it appears Trump has also been paying taxes in China—not a lot—but still more than he has been paying in the US.

have been changed for the next debate. Candidates will still be given two minutes to answer the moderator's questions, but as one person is answering, the other's microphone will be muted.

When the two minutes are up, both microphones will be on. It's unclear how this will work, but it I look forward to it. And I look forward to seeing how Trump handles himself.

So How Was the Debate?

It was interesting but not that exciting. Trump had obviously been schooled not to be such a dick this time, and for once, he took that advice. And for the most part, he did well. Biden, at times, tripped over his words but, overall, was composed—and, more importantly, credible.

The result? Polls were mixed. Some placed Biden as the clear winner and others, Trump, but I'm not sure whether the debate moved the needle either way. For me, it was honours even, perhaps with Biden just shading it.

Importantly, the Biden camp was at least happy he didn't screw up. Or did he? He said he was against fracking, preferring to move toward renewable energy. Great! But Pennsylvania, a key state, is in favour of fracking for the jobs it brings; so maybe that was not such a clever thing to say. Or maybe he could have expressed himself better. I hope it doesn't become more of an issue, but Biden did not have to go there.

Trump, to his credit, avoided the temptation to interrupt but still lied his balls off with almost every utterance, but who cares? His supporters love him—with or without balls!

More COVID at the White House as Trump and Biden Fight It Out

The weekend sees the two main protagonists out and about trying to get as many voters on their side as possible; but before they can even get their shoes on, we learn that at least five of Pence's aides, including his chief of staff, have contracted coronavirus!

It is utterly bewildering how the Shite House can be this stupid. The level of their ineptitude knows no bounds.

Anyway, Trump is not slowing down, and on Sunday, he manages three stopovers in the all-important Pennsylvania. But despite the surge in coronavirus cases, he still tells his crowds the corner has been turned and that the increase in numbers is attributable to more testing.

Of course, it makes no sense, but he has no choice but to stay with the same message. Any change would be seen as an about turn; but what is even more crazy is that when he spouts this nonsense at his rallies, the crowds love it. And as hard as I try, I just do not understand it.

Biden's schedule is nowhere near as full as Trump's, and he is receiving what many agree is justifiable criticism for not doing more.[13] On his travels, Biden is sticking to coronavirus as his leading theme; and he's been helped by a slipup from Mark Meadows, the White House chief of staff who said on Sunday, "We are not going to control the pandemic. We are going to control the fact that we get vaccines, therapeutics, and other mitigation areas." Wonderful stuff!

Pence, ignoring CDC guidelines to self-isolate, and Harris are also out doing their bit over the weekend. Frankly, neither is particularly impressive. Pence jogs his way off Air Force 2 like a Pinocchio puppet and dedicates his entire speech to arse-kissing Chump.

Harris, on the other hand, does not seem on top of things. I actually wonder if she's had a "wee dram" before going on stage because she doesn't seem focused and giggles a lot. But maybe I'm wrong as nothing is said in the press about her performance. Even Fox doesn't pick up on it, but they probably weren't covering it anyway.

---

[13] After losing the last election, Hillary Clinton received criticism for not campaigning enough in some of the key states; but Biden is doing even less at the moment, which is ringing alarm bells for some. OK, we have COVID-19, and it's surging. But that's not stopping Trump; he's doing more.

I wondered earlier whether Trump was throwing a Hail Mary by holding public rallies with coronavirus cases rising so much, but I don't think he is. He's simply doing what he thinks is necessary to win again. It worked last time, and anyway, he doesn't have much choice.

Trump Walks Out of 60 Minutes Interview

Early in the week, Trump has an interview with Lesley Stahl aired on CBS on Sunday, 25 October, but his performance is poor. Stahl, a highly experienced and respected journalist, starts by asking Trump if he is ready for tough questions.

Well, clearly he isn't. He dodges, ducks, dives, and lies; but Stahl is not deterred. Trump tells her that her questions should be fair. They are very fair, but he just doesn't like them and accuses all journalists of being much softer on Biden.

The interview covers masks, rallies, Fauci, and more, including why he still insists on bringing up Hillary Clinton. It's hard to believe we are watching the president of the US.

He struggles with healthcare questions. He has been promising a new plan since before he was elected and still nothing. According to KHN, a nonprofit news service covering health issues, "Trump has promised an Obamacare replacement plan five times so far this year. And the plan is always said to be just a few weeks away."

As the interview progresses, he becomes more frustrated with the questions and starts to complain. One short section is a lot of fun:

> STAHL. Do you know what you told me a long
>   time ago when I asked why you keep say-
>   ing "fake media"?
> TRUMP. Yeah? Yeah?
> STAHL. You said to me, "I say that because I
>   need to discredit you so that when you

say negative things about me, no one will believe you."

TRUMP. I don't have to discredit you.

STAHL. But that's what you told me.

TRUMP. You've discredited yourself.

STAHL. You know, I didn't want to have this kind of angry—

TRUMP. Of course you did.

STAHL. No, I didn't—

TRUMP. Of course you did—

STAHL. No, I didn't.

TRUMP. Well then, you brought up a lot of subjects that were inappropriately brought up—

STAHL. Well, I said, I'm gonna ask you tough questions. But—

TRUMP. They were inappropriately brought up right from the beginning. No, your first question was, "This is going to be tough questions." You don't ask Joe Biden. I saw your interview with Joe, the interview with Joe Biden.

STAHL. I never did a Joe Biden interview—

Shortly after that exchange, Honest Don has had enough and walks out with fifteen minutes still to go. A few minutes later, Kayleigh McEnany the White House press secretary, comes back with Trump's healthcare plan.

CBS later said of the plan, "It was heavy, filled with executive orders, congressional initiatives, but no comprehensive health plan."

27 October: On the Road Again

Biden is off to Georgia today looking to pick up that state's sixteen electoral votes. Georgia was last won by Democrats in

1992 by Bill Clinton, but the polls show Trump and Biden neck and neck. It will be an amazing win if Biden pulls it off. Trump won it by five points in 2016.

Meanwhile, Porky Pres is concentrating on the key states of Nebraska (five votes), Michigan (sixteen), and Wisconsin (twenty), where Biden is slightly ahead but not hugely so.

Obama is out again, this time in Orlando, Florida; and he delivers a similar speech to the one delivered in Pennsylvania. So not much more to add. But this time, he is more on the attack than last time.

It is unprecedented for a past president to criticise an incumbent in the way Obama is going after Trump, but I am reminded of the title of a song written by Bob Dylan in the 1960s, "The Times, They Are a-Changin.'"

Obama repeats a Michelle Obama line: "Being president doesn't change who you are—it reveals who you are."

He says that Trump is "jealous" of COVID because it gets more coverage than he does! Trump was watching Obama's speech on Fox News, and Obama clearly got to him. Talking with reporters later, he says, "Fox is very disappointing that they would put on this. This would not have happened with Roger Ailes."

What? Dodgy Don's buddy, Roger Ailes, was a former CEO and chairman of Fox News, who was forced to resign in 2016 following allegations of sexual assault by twenty-three women. Peas in a pod!

Kushner Confirms His Ignorance

Before getting to the latest round of Kush-crap, I'll take a quick trip back in time to when New York was struggling to cope with all COVID was throwing at it. According to *Vanity Fair*, Kushner, who had been charged with the responsibility of sorting out the "PPE mess," (Personal Protective Equipment) met with a group of business leaders on 21 March.

They were expecting to learn how they could help with the supply of PPE. Instead, Kushner says, "The federal government is not going to lead this response. It's up to the states to figure out what they want to do."

Then, in response to someone reportedly referring to a CNN article about Governor Andrew Cuomo's calls for help with supplies, Kushner calls it "CNN bullshit." He is also reported to have added, "Cuomo didn't pound the phones hard enough to get PPE for his state. His people are going to suffer, and that's their problem." Like father(-in-law), like idiot!

We shouldn't be surprised by this behaviour as Kushner is incompetent. He is unqualified to resolve this problem, and he is out of touch with reality.

It shows how he views everything through a political lens with no recognition that this is a nationwide problem affecting Democrats and Republicans alike. He completely misses the point and, worse, completely misses the opportunity that the business leaders were there saying, "How can we help?"

Back to today—sort of. While writing his book, *Rage*, Bob Woodward also recorded discussions with Kushner; and CNN has just got hold of a recording made on 18 April.

He tells Woodward that Trump is "getting the country back from the doctors" in what he calls a "negotiated settlement," whatever that is. Bear in mind this is mid-April, and we know that Trump is fully aware how dangerous coronavirus is but is determined to open the country up as he believes that will be good for his popularity. Kushy says Trump is "going to own the open-up."

Kushner tries to give the impression he's intelligent and that he has some idea what he's talking about but fails miserably at the first hurdle when he says a pandemic has three phases. "There's the panic phase, the pain phase, and then the comeback phase." Adding that the country was at the "beginning of the comeback phase." Whaaaaat?

Glad we got that cleared up, but he forgot to mention the "screw-up phase" and the "I-don't-know-what-the-fuck-I'm-doing phase." To be fair, he did indirectly mention the screw-up phase when he said, "Trump's now back in charge. It's not the doctors." And we already know Trump doesn't know what he's doing. So we're all good!

There are other gems, such as when, without realising, he refers to himself. He says, "The most dangerous people around the president are overconfident idiots," Luckily, Trump has "gotten rid of" these idiots (bar one, apparently!) and replaced them with "a lot more thoughtful people who kind of know their place and know what to do."

Kushner calls political parties "collections of tribes" and describes the pre-Trump Republican Party as a "collection of a bunch of tribes," but apparently that didn't last long as he says of Trump, "He basically did a full hostile takeover of the Republican Party." Doesn't that just warm the cockles of your heart?

And doesn't it tell you all you need to know about Trump's agenda?

Not to Be Outdone...

30 October: Possibly jealous of Jared getting all that publicity, Tweedledumb decides he will put in his two pennies' worth and goes on Fox to prove he can be just as stupid as the Kush.

When another record is broken, with nearly ninety thousand new coronavirus cases, he proclaims the rise in cases is because of testing, and he has the proof. See, he's executive vice president of The Trump Organization, so that means he's clever.

Yeah, Junior has been studying the CDC data very carefully to find out why the media only talks about cases and not deaths. He's so clever that he already has the answer and wants to share his discovery. Rhetorically, he asks, "Why aren't they talking about deaths? Oh! Oh! Because the number is almost nothing."

I told you he's clever! And to reassure us, he adds, "We've gotten control of this thing. We understand how it works…"

Un-bloody-believable! Yesterday, there were one thousand deaths in this country, you feckless moron.

It's a Race to the Finishing Line

Well, Biden may have been a bit slow off the mark, but he's now going at it hammer and tongs, matching Trump rally for rally. He is even matching Trump's three, and now four, stops a day.

He seems to be performing better with each rally, and it's encouraging to see that Kamala Harris has now hit her stride. She's passionate, measured, and believable—just what is needed. It is extremely tense, and I can't wait for the clock to move forward.

Whilst I believe Biden will win, I am fearful Trump might "trump" him. Biden is ahead in the national poll, but we know that's meaningless. And I get irritated that these numbers continue to be quoted.

In the individual states, he is ahead a couple of points here, a couple of points there—but will it be enough? This is nerve-wracking stuff, but you have to admire both Trump and Biden for their stamina. This breakneck schedule is certainly not for everyone.

Trump Again Questions Mail-In Ballots and More

An unprecedented number of people have taken advantage of early voting opportunities across the country, and a majority are believed to be Democrats. So far, early voters number an unprecedented ninety-three million and counting, of which sixty-one million by mail and thirty-two million in person, which is more than two-thirds of total votes cast at the last election.

This has prompted Trump to create confusion and mistrust in the process and in the system. In a number of states, the final result is not known on the day of the election as votes continue to be counted in the following days.

Some states don't even look at mail-in votes until the polling stations close and allow the counting of mail-in votes received a few days after Election Day, provided they are postmarked before Election Day.

Trump is looking for ways to halt or limit the counting of those votes. Michigan and Pennsylvania are among a number of states who say the final result may not be known for a few days.

Republicans are already challenging the right of some of these states to continue counting, and the Supreme Court has already ruled on two cases. Last week, on Wednesday, it allowed election officials in two battleground states, Pennsylvania and North Carolina, to accept absentee ballots for several days after Election Day.

Another case is being fought in Texas, where Republicans are trying to have some 170,000 drive-in votes from Harris County thrown out on the grounds that drive-in voting violates the US Constitution. No, it doesn't!

All of this suggests that if should Trump lose, he is trying to keep the Democratic majority as small as possible so he can take it to the Supreme Court, which, thanks to the addition of Amy Barrett, means it's now stacked with Republicans.

On the subject of Barrett, I had thought the Senate hearings over her accession to the Supreme Court would have been a fun spectacle, especially with the prospect of Kamala Harris questioning her, but it was all rather dull.

Harris was much less prosecutorial than usual. Perhaps because she is a potential vice president, she was more circumspect. The hearings can best be summed up as: Comey Barrett was asked questions. She evaded. She was asked more questions. She avoided. She got sworn in!

A Review of COVID-19 Cases in the US

I'll end the month with a look at some numbers, which yet again are disappointing. In the space of one month, new cases per day have almost doubled from forty-two thousand to eighty-one thousand, pushing total cases up by 2 million to 9.2 million.

As disappointing as these numbers are, we can take encouragement, if that's the right word, from a less sharp increase in deaths when compared to case numbers, which are now at 850 a day compared to 720 a month ago. This certainly reflects improved treatment methods.

One area of concern is that a number of states are reporting higher positivity rates, and with the onset of the flu season, we have to hope the increase in case numbers is not a harbinger of worse to come.

November 2020

Not Long Now...

Waiting for the election bell to ring is nerve-wracking beyond belief. In the red corner, Trump manages ten rallies in two days. In the blue corner, Biden manages seven. It's a hectic pace for both of them, and no matter what your views, they have to be admired.

Biden stays on theme and continues to bang the unity and coronavirus drums. Trump also remains true to form by lying with every breath he takes. It's extraordinary. No matter what he says, his fans lap it up. He's like a conductor, orchestrating every boo and every cheer. I doubt we'll ever see a president like him again.

I certainly hope not.

3 November—The United States Presidential Election

Finally, the day has arrived, and everyone is filled with a combination of excitement and nervous apprehension. And we learn a record 101 million early votes have been cast, setting up the possibility of a record turnout for a presidential election.

Trump appears on Fox and Friends and says he will claim victory "when there is victory, if there is victory." Not quite sure what that means.

Biden appears confident and is looking to win Texas, thirty-eight Electoral College votes; North Carolina, fifteen; and Arizona, eleven; and to win back Wisconsin, ten; Michigan, sixteen; Pennsylvania, twenty; and Florida, twenty-nine.

Victories are traded throughout the day with results going as expected; however, Biden suffers big disappointments in losing Florida and Texas, despite narrowing the 2016 gaps. It's clear there will be no early indication of a winner, let alone a result, but Biden is making no inroads. In fact, quite the contrary.

My day ends with Trump well ahead in Biden's key states of Pennsylvania, Wisconsin, and Michigan.

Biden is ahead on electoral votes, but this is not looking good. The TV gurus tell us not to worry. Republicans like to vote in person, so we see their numbers first, and Democrats prefer to vote early by mail. So wait until tomorrow as the mail-in votes are counted—the numbers should change. I hope so. I'm off to bed!

I wake to learn that Trump, in an unhinged announcement, declared victory at two thirty in the morning. He ranted:

> Millions and millions of people voted for us tonight, and a very sad group of people is trying to disenfranchise that group of people. And we won't stand for it. We will not stand for it. And did I predict this, did I say this? I've been saying this from the day I heard they were going to send out tens of millions of ballots because either they were going to win or, if they didn't win, they'll take us to court.

He added,

> This is a fraud on the American public. This is an embarrassment to our country. We were getting ready to win this election. Frankly, we did win this election. So our goal now is to ensure the integrity—for the good of this nation. This is a very big moment. This is a major fraud on our nation.

Things are now playing out in line with our worst fears, and Trump goes on to say, "We want the law to be used in a proper manner, so we'll be going to the US Supreme Court. We want all voting to stop. We don't want them to find any ballots at four o'clock in the morning and add them to the list. OK? It's a very sad moment."

And if that wasn't enough, he added, "We will win this, and as far as I'm concerned, we already have won it."

What a twenty-four-carat nutcase! His rant was widely condemned—by Democrats, Republicans and even Fox!

But How Are Things Going?

Despite Biden leading Loopy Lou by 238 to 213 electoral votes, it does not look good. Trump leads by 600,000-plus votes in Pennsylvania (20 electoral votes), and he's well ahead in Michigan (16) and Wisconsin (10). Wins here would take him to 259 votes, just 11 away from victory; but when you add in North Carolina (15), which is a near certainty, it's game over for Biden.

But what about the TV gurus? It turns out they may have been right as in no time, the lead in Pennsylvania is cut to 500,000. Not bad. Biden also narrows the gaps in Wisconsin and Michigan. Even better! As the day progresses, Biden closes in on both Michigan and Wisconsin and then overtakes Trump and then wins those states. Done! Twenty-six more votes for Biden. I never doubted it!

Other states in play are Georgia (16), Arizona (11), and Nevada (6). This is unexpected. Biden had a razor-thin lead in Nevada overnight, and that remains the same all day as frustratingly there are no updates.

Georgia was never thought to be in play for Biden. A couple of days ago, he was around 600,000 votes adrift, but that is changing. We shall see. Tonight, I go to bed much happier than last night, and I look forward to waking up to further positive developments—Biden 253, Trump 213.

5 November: One Hundred Thousand Coronavirus Cases in One Day

For the first time in any country, coronavirus cases exceeded 100,000 in a single day. At the end of June, Dr. Fauci warned 100,000 cases a day was possible if we didn't change our behaviour, but he was not taken seriously as numbers at that time were 60,000 to 70,000 a day. It's sad that he would be proven right.

But we are not alone. Cases in many parts of the world are on the rise. We even see that Germany, France, and England have reintroduced lockdown conditions; and Italy has put some regions on red alert. We all knew a second wave would come, but it looks like we've done nothing to prepare for it.

The prospect of New York going back into lockdown is not one I relish. However, I'm proud of everyone in Manhattan. When I go out, the vast majority of people still wear masks; and even though there are so many new cases in the country, Manhattan, with a population density of 74,000 per square mile[14] (1.7 million people in twenty-three square miles) has only 121 new cases.

Case numbers will certainly increase, but at least we start from a low base—something indeed to be proud of.

Biden Pushes On…

After a restful night, there are no changes in electoral votes won, but as the day unfolds, Biden continues to eat into Trump's lead. A large majority of all the mail-in votes are cast in favour of Biden, and it is looking increasingly possible that Biden will achieve a rare win over an incumbent president.

As each hour passes, it even looks possible he will win Georgia, Pennsylvania, Arizona, and Nevada, which together will give Biden 306 electoral votes, exactly the same number achieved by Trump in 2016. A nice irony.

---

[14] For comparison, the population density in Greater London is 15,000 per square mile.

In the evening, Trump makes an announcement in the White House briefing room. He devotes his time to moaning about how he is losing because of votes illegally cast, so he's not really losing. He's winning. Absolutely pathetic!

Events he describes sound like he is referring to a completely different election. He accuses the Democrats of all sorts of wrongdoings and talks of multiple lawsuits to right all the wrongs. Staggering!

This man is president of the United States, and this is how he performs. It's tragic. It's pitiful. He's like a spoilt child. He is so driven by his ego that he doesn't even realise his words will live in perpetuity.

Despite Trump, I go to bed with a sense of joy, knowing that barring a miracle, Biden will become the next president of the United States, but also with sadness that Trump ever held this office in the first place.

It's getting better all the time. Friday morning reveals that Biden is in the lead in Georgia, Pennsylvania, Arizona and Nevada. It's now certain Biden will become the next president, but mathematically, Trump can still win. So he cannot yet be declared the winner. But fear not—it's only a matter of time.

Biden Wins!

Biden is declared the winner on the morning of Saturday, 7 November!

Donald Trump, you're *fired*!

But What About Trump's Legacy?

One-term Trump! I cannot say how happy I am. He now becomes only the fourth one-term president in modern times.[15] It is such a great feeling to write knowing Trump is on his way out.

---

[15] The other modern-time one-term presidents were Herbert Hoover, 1929–1933; Jimmy Carter, 1977–1981; and George H. W. Bush 1989–1993.

When he first became president, I was shocked but hoped his crude behaviour would be tempered as he settled into office, but I was sadly wrong. It got worse. He abused the office he held and abused anyone who disagreed with him or challenged him in any way.

He turned the White House into the Shite House, and he should never be forgiven the way he managed the coronavirus. His mismanagement of the pandemic is directly responsible for the deaths of thousands upon thousands of people.

He leaves office, leaving a mess behind him—a mess that will take years to put right. But at least he's leaving!

He appointed his idiot family members to positions they had neither the right nor the competence to hold. Ivanka Trump, advisor to the president? Are you serious? Kushner, senior advisor to the president? Which idiot thought that was a good idea?

And what about Tweedledumb and Tweedledumber? They had no formal positions but were still thrown in front of the cameras to spout their nonsense. All of them are jokes, and it will be great to see the back of them.

But what about Trump's achievements? He falsely claims credit for everything positive, including the economic growth in his first three years, but in fairness, he did take positive steps to cut down on bureaucracy.

Shortly after assuming office, he directed all fifteen of the departments of the federal government to submit plans within six months to streamline and modernise their operations. That was indeed a success.

Another achievement, without realising it, was to draw attention the increasing gulf between rich and poor in this country, and it is typically from the less well-off that he gets his support.

It will be crucial that Biden listens to the concerns of these people. He talks about being president to all Americans, and he needs to be sure to keep his word on that. Increasing taxes may be part of the solution, but he should not push forward too hard nor too soon.

As much as I dislike Trump, and ignoring those on the far right, I do feel sorry for many of his supporters because they've been duped. He has managed to get them so fired up that no matter what he says, they believe him, and they know that no matter what they do, he will never condemn them.

Trump made a number of promises, but they barely affected the blue-collar workers of his base. He promised to reduce corporation tax—done. He promised to leave the Paris Agreement on climate change—done. He promised more judges—he appointed masses of lower-court judges and three Supreme Court justices—definitely done. He moved the American embassy from Tel Aviv to Jerusalem—done.[16]

He also tackled trade with China, essentially saying that the US always got the short end of the stick. He was right to do this, and he was right when he said it should have been done long ago. But he was completely wrong to go it alone.

He could easily have looked at tackling the problem in conjunction with allies, but that's not his style. And it's a massive fundamental failing of his. A joint effort would have had far more affect, but from day 1 of his presidency, Trump was more interested in distancing himself from his allies, rather than embracing them.

But what about the promises he didn't keep, particularly those aimed at his base? He promised to build a border wall, which Mexico—a country full of "rapists and murderers"—would pay for. He promised to deport all "11.3 million" illegal immigrants. He actually deported less people than Obama, even if the 11.3 million number was a fabrication.

He promised to rebuild infrastructure, "putting millions of people back to work." He didn't even get started. He promised to restore the failing coal industry, which made him super popular

---

[16] Previous presidents, Obama, Bush, and Clinton had repeatedly sidestepped the issue by deferring the decision every six months; but according to the BBC, Trump faced a lot of pressure from parts of his base, including right-wing American Jews whose message was pushed by conservative Orthodox Jews dominating Trump's inner circle, as well as one Paula White, but more on her later.

in places like Wyoming, West Virginia and Pennsylvania. It did not happen, but it was always a nonstarter. It would have been a mistake anyway.

But all this apart, they still support him. Why? I think it's just that as his rhetoric increases the divide in the country, so each side becomes more entrenched in its beliefs. Divide and rule! However, it also shows he holds his base in contempt.

He deliberately lies to them and repeats conspiracy theories, knowing they will believe him, and that's all that matters. And even better, the more they believe him, the more license he is given for even more ridiculous utterings. And so it goes.

In 2015, Hillary called his supporters "the deplorables." He probably agrees; in fact, I would not be at all surprised if he holds them in even more contempt than Hillary.

But What about the Future?

Biden is setting the tone by saying he will not be a president for red states or blue states but the United States. He is setting down his marker that he can work across the aisle, and this looks increasingly necessary as the Democrats manage to lose seats in the House of Representatives but squeak through with a reduced majority. And they may well not gain the Senate as they had hoped.

We will know on 5 January who controls the Senate after runoff elections take place in Georgia for its two seats as they will determine the majority.

How can this happen when Democrats were apparently so confident of holding the House and winning the Senate? Simple. Sometimes the Democrats are so stupid that they manage to clutch defeat from the jaws of victory.

Extolling the virtues of socialism and supporting defunding the police may well reflect views of so-called progressives, but it does not help win House and Senate seats and does not comport with the views of the majority centrists in the Democratic Party.

It's great to be true to your morals and principles, but you also need to use your brain. It's much easier to influence change from the inside. On the outside, the most you can do is make a nuisance of yourself as you wait for the next election to come round, giving you another opportunity to screw things up.

If the Republicans win even one of the Georgia seats, they will retain the Senate, and Biden's success at the polls will amount to no more than a Pyrrhic victory. He will face a constant uphill battle to push forward any of his agenda. Democrats need both seats to reach fifty-fifty in the Senate, in which case, Vice President Kamala Harris has the casting vote.

The far left may well have a lot to answer for. So far they have been really stupid. Being smart is one thing, but if you lack common sense, you're no more than an educated idiot.

But What Is Defunding the Police?

Defunding the police means different things to different people. For the Looney Left, it seems to mean getting rid of the police altogether and replacing them with a bunch of tree huggers—or some such bollocks, but to others, it means reviewing the role of the police and making reforms where necessary. But let's be clear. Only 20 percent of Americans support the Looney Left notions.

Of course we should not defund the police, but equally obvious is that reform is needed. We need the police!

But what to do? First, this country needs to admit to the reality of racism within the police force instead of paying lip service to the problems. Some officers are out-and-out racists and should be kicked off the force, but it's not always as easy as that. The police force often deals with difficult or underperforming personnel in the same way as many corporations: they transfer them somewhere else.

There needs to be a cultural change within the force. The purpose of law enforcement, after all, is "to promote public safety and uphold the rule of law so that individual liberty may flourish." And the vast majority of police officers that join the force do so because they genuinely want to serve.

However, when an officer steps out of line, he or she may well be reprimanded internally but is all too often wrapped in a protective "blue blanket." There is not enough transparency nor accountability, and that is precisely why police officers have gone unpunished for criminal actions. And that is why a number of people want the police defunded.

There is obviously no common solution for each of the fifty states, but the role of the police should definitely be reviewed. And a common thread of that review should result in them becoming more accessible, giving them more opportunity to interact with their local communities. They should receive more focused training and know with absolute certainty that they will be held accountable for their actions.

So what should be done? Apart from kicking the racists off the force and giving help to troubled officers, I don't have the answers, but nor does anyone else—or else it would already have been done. One ingredient so often missing in the relationship between police and the public is trust, particularly in cases where force is used and in fatal shootings. If those issues alone were tackled, it would be a start. What about establishing external review boards to look into such cases?

Ironically, perhaps the call to defund the police is not such a bad thing because if nothing else, it has brought the need for reform to the fore. Whatever changes are made, they will not happen quickly, but they should be done in cooperation with the local community so everyone knows what they can expect from their polices officers. Doing nothing is itself an action—a bad one.

Fun-Day Monday, 9 November

It was a quiet weekend, apart from Trump still refusing to concede victory to Biden and going ahead with his lawsuits. Of course, we still had Tosser Ted Cruz and Loser Lindsey Graham, expressing their support of Trump's Canute-like fight against the election tide.

One of Biden's first actions is to announce the formation of his own task force to fight coronavirus. He lays out how he will follow science but wants more PPE and more testing.

He urges Americans to stop looking at mask-wearing as political but instead to wear one for the sake of others, saying that a mask "is the most potent weapon" against the virus. What a difference. Biden shows genuine empathy, understanding, and concern; and even better, he makes sense. After the lies and bombast of Trump, listening to Biden is somewhat reassuring.

It would be great if he could remove the politics from the pandemic, especially as today, after six hundred thousand COVID cases in the last five days, the grim milestone of ten million is passed.

But maybe this black cloud has a silver lining: Pfizer's chairman and CEO, Albert Bourla, announces today that interim analysis shows Pfizer/BioNTech's candidate vaccine has proven well over 90 percent effective in global trials.

The trials are to continue into December, but as *The Guardian* says, "The headline results were emphatic," adding, "Regulators will be looking to process an emergency licence application at record speed." Everybody is over the moon at the prospect of a vaccination by summer(ish) next year.

It should come as no surprise Pfizer's announcement caused a worldwide surge in stocks, and the Dow (the exchange Trump uses as a bellwether for his brilliant management of the economy) opened above that all-important 29,500 level, albeit closing lower. I love it, but given the way the Dow now performs, perhaps it should be renamed the COVID Index.

Trump can no longer associate himself with any positive moves in the Dow; but that doesn't stop number-one son, Tweedledumb, from questioning Pfizer's integrity, suggesting there's something "nefarious about the timing of this." It gets better all the time!

What is not getting better are the actions taken by Attorney General Bill Barr. Since his appointment, he has acted as Trump's personal attorney, and that doesn't change as today he authorises prosecutors to look into allegations of voting irregularities. What irregularities?

This is an extraordinary move as no evidence has been offered in support of any allegation, but it does allow Trump to continue to withhold his concession to Biden, thus making things even more difficult for the incoming president. Right now, I feel I'm living in Cuckoo Land.

But there is hope. Neil Cavuto, a Fox News host, is an unusual person in that he is prepared to challenge One-Term. *The Daily Beast* writes that Cavuto told people in May not to take hydroxy-chloroquine, saying, "This will kill you," that he interrupted a Trump speech to fact-check false claims One-Term was making about Obama's record, and that he gave Education Secretary Betsy de Vos a hard time over her "reckless" plan to reopen schools during the pandemic.

But he does even better today. At a White House press conference, Kayleigh McEnany alleges electoral fraud, causing Cavuto immediately to cut into the broadcast, saying, "Whoa… I just think we have to be very clear. She's charging that the other side is welcoming fraud and welcoming illegal voting. Unless she has more details to back that up, I can't, in good countenance, continue showing you this."

This is pretty impressive, but Cavuto isn't finished and goes on, "Maybe they do have something else to back that up, but that's an explosive charge to make, that the other side is effectively rigging and cheating." He promises to return to the press conference if McEnany provides proof, which she doesn't. Cavuto wraps the section up by saying, "Not so fast." Nice one, Mr. Cavuto!

Veterans Day—Wednesday, 11 November 2020

Today is US Veterans Day, a day when those who lost their lives in all wars are remembered. In the UK today, as in France, it is called Remembrance Day, the history of which marks the end of hostilities in WWI. Officially the war ended when the Treaty of Versailles was signed on 28 June 1919.

However, it wasn't until much later when the Allies and Germany put into effect an armistice on the "eleventh hour of the eleventh day of the eleventh month." On Remembrance Day, we Brits observe one minute's silence at eleven o'clock, in memory of lives lost in all conflicts, and commemorate it by ceremony and by wearing poppies.

Originally, Veterans Day was known as Armistice Day, but after WWII and the Korean War and following pressure from veterans service organisations, Congress amended the commemoration in June 1954 by changing the word *armistice* to *veterans* so the day would honour American veterans of all wars.

So today, both Trump and Biden carry out their responsibilities as party leaders, honouring all servicemen and women; but for Trump, this is the first time he is seen in public for five or six days. For a change, he has nothing to say! Paradise! It's so good not to hear his bullshit, especially today.

Still No Concession

As Trump continues his refusal to concede victory to Joe Biden, Biden continues to be denied access to the president's daily briefing, a highly classified daily report dealing with the country's most sensitive intelligence.

CNN reports that Trump is also denying Biden access to State Department resources. This is another childish act. The State Department normally supports international operations of the president-elect; and according to CNN, for that reason, world leaders typically send their congratulatory messages through that department. So denying Biden access to those messages means he is forced to forge his own path.

On 15 November, Trump tweets something that suggests he may be on the brink of a concession, saying about Biden,

> He won because the Election was Rigged, NO VOTE WATCHERS OR OBSERVERS allowed, vote tabulated by a Radical Left pri-

vately owned company, Dominion, with a bad reputation & bum equipment that couldn't even qualify for Texas (which I won by a lot!), the Fake & Silent Media, & more!

Alas, not long after, probably as a result of the reaction he got to beginning his tweet with "He won…" he writes again, this time saying, "RIGGED ELECTION. WE WILL WIN! He only won in the eyes of the FAKE NEWS MEDIA. I concede NOTHING! We have a long way to go. This was a RIGGED ELECTION!" This is pathetic and beyond belief. Trump is certifiable.

Earlier, on Friday, nine of the cases brought by Trump's lawyers are either rejected or dropped. One judge even described the evidence submitted as "inadmissible hearsay within hearsay," but still Trump persists. Also on Friday, some of Trump's lawyers decide to throw in the towel and resign. It's impossible to make this stuff up!

So following Fatty's Friday failure, he appoints ridiculous Rudy Giuliani, who's not even a courtroom lawyer, to head his legal challenges. This should be fun as you can be sure that Rudy, who is as big a stranger to the truth as Trump, can be totally relied on to transform this nonsense from farce to fiasco!

Million MAGA March

On Saturday, 14 November, Trump supporters hold a rally in Washington, DC, the "Million MAGA March," to protest the election results. Attendance is difficult to measure but is judged to exceed the ten thousand predicted.

As the day unfolds, we finally get to understand why Trump fans believe they won the election. It's because they can't count. Kayleigh McEnany, White House secretary, tweets, "More than one MILLION marchers for President descend on the swamp in support." A great example of Trumpian truth!

Sunday draws to a close with the US passing the eleven million coronavirus case mark. Deaths are approaching 250,000, and hospitalisations are at record levels. This is heartbreaking. It has taken a mere six days to go from ten million cases to eleven million. Can you believe it? Of course you can. But what does One-Term have to say on the subject? "The election was rigged."

The biggest fear about the rising case numbers is that with Thanksgiving, Christmas, and the New Year around the corner, family celebrations will cause all numbers to grow further. A compounding worry is that as treatment methods continue to improve, some people now seem to regard COVID as less life-threatening and are therefore less cautious. These are real worries.

As a final, happy, and unrelated note on this Sunday, 15 November, SpaceX makes history with the launching of its Crew Dragon spacecraft from the Kennedy Space Center in Florida with four astronauts on board on their way to the space station. They will spend about six months on board, conducting various science experiments, as well as carrying out updates and repairs on the space station. Good luck to them. We may all be joining them soon!

Coronavirus—Stronger than Ever

Is it getting out of control? Coronavirus cases have exceeded one hundred thousand for each of the last fourteen days.[17] And positivity rates reported by Johns Hopkins as of 16 November show an alarming rise in a number of states:

Kansas	58.7 percent
South Dakota	58.4 percent
Iowa	50.7 percent
Wyoming	44.6 percent
Idaho	40.2 percent

---

[17] One hundred thousand cases a day, and much more, were to continue for the remainder of the year and beyond.

These numbers are literally unbelievable. Case numbers are breaking record levels every day. Hospitalisations are currently at seventy-three thousand, another record, and the number of deaths marches inexorably upward. As the positivity rates are seven-day moving averages, we know they are set to deteriorate further in many more states.

The problem has continued to be dealt with on political lines; and this is no better demonstrated than in Iowa, population 3.15 million, where Governor Kim Reynolds, a devoted Trump ally, has consistently refused to support mask-wearing mandates, dismissing them as "feel-good" measures.

Even at the beginning of November when Iowa had one of the highest positivity rates, she still resisted. But guess what? Now that the shit is really hitting the fan, she supports mask-wearing and other protective measures. Some may say, "Better late than never," but it's certainly too late for the more than two thousand Iowans who have already lost their lives. What a fool.

Aside from showing what a countrywide mess this is, the numbers clearly show the effect of incompetent crisis management. Give Trump a problem to solve, and he's guaranteed to balls it up every time. I am so happy this clown will soon no longer be president, and waking up each morning knowing that One-Term is on his way out means I start each day with a huge smile on my face.

Trump the Chump

The Orange One is really struggling to come to terms with the fact he lost the election, 306 to 232 electoral votes—exactly the same margin he won by, which he called a "landslide" and said he had given Hillary a "shellacking"! He can't deal with it.

It's now fifteen days after the election, and he still won't concede to Biden. And tellingly, only about three Republicans have had the courage publicly to accept Biden's victory.

So with all his boo-hoo emotions, last week, Chumpy had a bit of a tantrum and started firing people, most notable among whom was Defense Secretary Mark Esper. But his termination, announced on Twitter, was not totally unexpected. By the way, Esper now joins the ranks of a number of people who have been FBT'd (fired by tweet) by Trump.

Esper had crossed swords a couple of times with One-Term, so he was always likely to be in the "firing" line. In Esper's place, Trump appointed a yes-man, one Christopher Miller. Trump avoids lengthy approval processes of many of his appointees by making them "acting" or "interim." Miller is interim defense secretary.

Esper was not happy with the walk to the church back in June. He thought he was going to "see some damage and to talk to the troops" and had no idea protesters were forcefully cleared from Lafayette Square so Trump could have his photo taken by the church.

Esper was also against bringing back troops from Iraq and Afghanistan, but interim is not. So with Esper out of the way, Miller announces the withdrawal of 2,500 troops from Iraq and 2,500 from Afghanistan, approximately halving the total in each country.

This will happen on 15 January 2021, just five days before Biden is inaugurated as the country's forty-sixth president. Miller gave no details about who was leaving or who was staying or why. But who cares? Job done!

Someone else who got up Trump's nose was Christopher Krebs, a highly respected top cybersecurity official. Krebs headed the little known Cybersecurity and Infrastructure Security Agency (CISA), which comes under the Department of Homeland Security and is, in this context, responsible for monitoring and overseeing that there is no hanky-panky in the election.

Trump got fed up with Krebs tweeting and messaging that the election was fair and properly conducted. Perhaps the tweet that really got to Trump was Krebs citing fifty-nine election security agents, saying there was no credible evidence of computer fraud in the election outcome.

Less than two hours later, Krebs became another FBT victim when Trump tweeted, "Effective immediately, Chris Krebs has been terminated as director of the Cybersecurity and Infrastructure Agency." Great, you get fired for telling the truth.

Mayor de Blasio Closes Public Schools in New York

After all the concerns about the opening of schools across the country, the result was that it proved to be pretty successful. There was no mad nationwide rush to reopen; but instead, local authorities, where schools did open, thought through what they needed to do and implemented a range of safety measures to protect children and teachers alike.

In many ways, it was an object lesson to all, demonstrating that when it comes to our children, we are neither Republican nor Democrat. There have been a few COVID outbreaks at schools and colleges around the country, but they were due more to the excesses of older students than a failing of protection measures.

In contrast, here in New York, Mayor Bill de Blasio announces that on Thursday, 19 November, all public schools will be closed due to the rise in coronavirus cases. This comes about because the city has reached a seven-day average positivity rate of 3 percent. Yes, 3 percent!

This is not a popular decision, especially given what's happening in the rest of the country, but case numbers are going up in New York and will no doubt continue to do so. More measures, such as closing gyms and banning indoor dining, are reportedly under consideration by Governor Cuomo.

I get that a limit was set and has been broken, and for that reason, de Blasio wants to honour his commitment to parents. However, with all the advances made in the treatment of coronavirus, parents are struggling to understand why their children can't go to school where they wear masks, but they can go to restaurants where people don't.

This doesn't seem to have been thought through very carefully. Add to this, the good news that younger children have proven to be less susceptible to contracting coronavirus could mean the children will be back at school soon, but much is likely to depend on the rate of new infections.

Whatever happens, every effort should be made to ensure that when schools do reopen, there is no repeat of this. One additional measure that would give comfort all-round is in-school rapid testing, but that is still some way off.

Less uncertain is the prospect of vaccines, which now gives real hope for next year. Knuckling down for a bit longer makes the vaccine a prize worth pushing for. Easy for me to say—I don't have school-age children to worry about.

Some Thoughts on Congress, Religion, and More

The appointment of Amy Barrett to the Supreme Court was an appointment based on faith, and I have no doubt in the years to come, we will see how the "religion of the right" may shape the country. However, amid all this turmoil, with Trump sitting at home sucking his thumb, it got me thinking about religion in Congress.

When I came to the US, I was struck by the number of politicians who brought God into the conversation when being interviewed, but I am not convinced about the conviction of most of them.

Maybe I'm naïve when it comes to religion, but I think believers of any faith should demonstrate a concern for humanity, a tolerance of others, and have a closeness to the truth, at the very least. But very few politicians tick those boxes.

Mike Pence is a good example. He is said to be deeply religious and describes himself as a "born-again evangelical Catholic," whatever that is, so how does his faith manifest itself? First, he demonstrates his tolerance and his humanity by being against same-sex marriage.

Also, when governor of Indiana, he opposed efforts to relocate refugees on the grounds that they presented "security concerns," and he supported the right of businesses and individuals to refuse to do business with people based on their own religious beliefs. Seriously? These look more the beliefs of a bigot than a man of faith.

For another example, look no further than one of my favourite senators, Loser Lindsey Graham. At the end of October last year while campaigning in South Carolina, he added misogyny to the list of his many charms. A self-proclaimed "follower of Jesus," he said that if women want a place in America, they must oppose abortion, be religious, and "follow traditional family structure." What a total arse. No wonder he's not married.

And I can't help but mention Tosser Ted Cruz. When it comes to religion—and everything else for that matter—he is among the very best of hypocrites. He is perfect proof that believing in God does not mean you're a good person because even if he does believe in God, he is definitely not a good person.

He is a bend-with-the-wind politician, lying, saying and doing whatever is necessary to get votes or deflect criticism.

Even the evangelicals told him to take it down a notch in the Bible belt when his 2015 presidential campaign speeches were more like sermons. One of his lines of bullshit was that "any president who doesn't begin the day on his knees isn't fit to be commander-in-chief of this country." I can easily imagine Tosser Ted being on his knees each morning, if only to beg forgiveness for his sins of the previous day.

Being a believer, Ted knows that somebody important once commanded, "Thou shalt not kill." But despite that, Teddy Boy supports the death penalty, and that's OK because as he once said, "The majority of violent criminals are Democrats." If there is a God, Ted, may he have mercy on your soul—if you have one.

But to be clear, not all politicians are like that. Take for example John Kasich, former Republican governor of Ohio and a 2015 candidate for presidential nominee. He regularly refers to his faith when speaking but doesn't use it in a way to show everyone what a good chap he is. He speaks from his heart and to his faith.

Another positive example is Mitt Romney, who Joe Biden has described as "a man of enormous integrity, who lives his faith."

Biden himself is deeply religious, but again he does not shout it from the rooftops.

According to a report by Pew Research Center in October 2019, the US is gradually becoming less religious.

In 2009, 17 percent of the population claimed not to be religious. In 2019, that percentage had increased to 26 percent, but within Congress, only one person (Democrat Jared Huffman) admitted to having no religious affiliation. Another eighteen were either don't-knows or refused to say, representing a total of only 3.5 percent of Congress.

So 26 percent of the population are not religious but only 3.5 percent of Congress. Having 96.5 percent of Congress claiming to be religious has to be statistically impossible. Anyway, they're politicians!

But no matter. It is unlikely anyone from Congress will ever admit to being atheist anytime soon because as Huffman rightly says, atheism brings with it "the notion of being anti-religion." So for the time being at least, members of Congress will perpetuate the notion that proportionately they are more religious than the rest of the country.

That's political expedience for you. And don't forget, even the Porky Pres professes piety. And for good measure, he has an evangelical advisory board, chaired by a screwball called Paula White.

She's a preacher and author, which is fine, but she's also a televangelist, which is not. Like most televangelists in the US, she's a proponent of some BS called "prosperity theology," which was described in a *Washington Post* article as long as eleven years ago as "insipid heresy" and as "pernicious doctrine."

It is the belief of a group of crackpot Protestant Christians that being rich and well is decided by God and if you want those things, then you must show your faith, speak positively, and, most importantly, donate lots of money to religious causes, such as those crazy churches established by—you've guessed it—televangelists!

White is a big fan of One-Term. In fact, she's such a big fan that in November 2019, she said that Trump's political opponents "operate in sorcery and witchcraft" and that "any persons [or] entities that are aligned against the president will be exposed and dealt with and overturned by the superior blood of Jesus."What a nutter!

But better than that, in early June this year, she decided it was up to her, single-handedly, to rid the world of coronavirus; so she spoke directly to the virus, saying, "We say it is enough. Die now, coronavirus 19!"

She then went on, "We command right now that this virus stop. There will be no more spread in the name of Jesus." Well, apparently Jesus wasn't listening as at that time, coronavirus cases were "only" about two million, compared to eighteen million, and rising, today!

She and Trump would make a great couple. He's delusional, and she's barking mad.

It Can't Get Any Worse! Or Can it?

I honestly believe Trump is losing it mentally—if he hasn't done so already. Having had the Georgia recount confirmed in Biden's favour, Trump turns to GOP lawmakers from Michigan in another effort to overturn the election result, seeking to get them to call Michigan in his favour. Biden won Michigan by a 155,000-vote margin, so what on earth does Wanknuts think he's doing?

But he may not be done with Georgia just yet. Under Georgia law, he can ask for another recount, and that's exactly what he does! Continuing to cry fraud and asking for the recount to be recounted may not be the best thing to do—it may just come back to bite Republicans in the arse.

If Georgia Republicans really do believe the fix is in as Dodgy Don says, they may even not bother voting at the Senate elections. So be careful, Dodgy!

Trump lawsuits continue apace and continue to fail or be withdrawn, but Rudy Giuliani promises there are yet more to come. Yesterday, 18 November, he gave one of the most deranged, craziest press conferences ever seen as he continued to allege widespread fraud all across the country.

"I know crimes. I can smell them," he said. "You don't have to smell this one. I can prove it to you eighteen different ways. I can prove to you that he won Pennsylvania by three hundred thousand votes. I can prove to you that he won Michigan probably fifty thousand votes."

Interesting that he mentioned Pennsylvania as when he was in court there, he was asked directly if he was alleging fraud. His reply? "No fraud." He can't say anything else because as Republican senator Ben Sasse points out, "When Trump campaign lawyers have stood before courts under oath, they have repeatedly refused to actually allege grand fraud—because there are legal consequences for lying to judges." Sasse is one of the few Republicans to have congratulated Biden on his victory.

What made Rudy's press conference even more bizarre was that he had apparently dyed his hair especially for the occasion. The problem was as he spoke, he was sweating brown streaks of perspiration down the sides of his face. As farcical as this is, this nonsense is being played out on the world stage, making a mockery of democracy in America.

In the meantime, good old Rudy seems determined to destroy the last vestige of whatever remains of his tattered reputation; and for once, he's doing a great job.

As for One-Term, he is desperately looking for ways to lay the blame for his loss at the doors of others. Based on the lack of evidence submitted to the courts, he knows his lawsuits will be fruitless, but he will never admit to losing—better to say he was robbed.

This man is so self-centred he doesn't care what effects his actions have on the country or its citizens. Oh yes, and still no word from him on COVID. As of 20 November, daily cases skyrocket, looking certain to hit two hundred thousand a day. Hospitalisations top eighty thousand; and deaths now exceed 2,000 a day, having already pushed through 250,000.

As an aside, we learn today that Tweedledumb and Andrew Giuliani, son of Ranting Rudy, have both tested positive for COVID. Kismet!

More Michigan Madness

When you get to the bottom of the barrel, keep scraping. At least that seems to be Trump's credo. Michigan GOP leaders met with Trump yesterday, after which they said they were not aware of any information that would change the outcome of the election in Michigan, so it was reasonable to assume the matter was closed. Wrong!

In an extraordinary move today, we learn the Republican National Committee, a separate body, asked for a two-week delay before certifying the state's election results as they want to audit the votes cast in Wayne County, the state's most populous county which includes Detroit.

But what's this all this about? Why audit a result which gave Biden 600,000 votes and Trump 270,000, a majority of 330,000—more than double the margin of the state victory?

Well, it's an audit, not a recount, and there is a suggestion this has racist overtones as Wayne County has a 38 percent Black population overall but 79 percent in Detroit. The objective appears to be to find a way to exclude majority-Black Detroit from the election certification in an attempt to give a victory to Trump.

Who could ever have imagined that officials charged with the responsibility of safeguarding the integrity of the US presidential election could stoop so low? This is beyond preposterous, but I'm sure their efforts will crumble to dust, along with their reputations. I hope.

In the end, all comes to naught, but it is unbelievable that this ridiculous notion ever found traction in the first place.

23 November: Trump Concedes—Sort Of!

Finally! But Trump still can't concede properly. In a tweet, he wrote, "I want to thank Emily Murphy at GSA for her stead-fast dedication and loyalty to our Country. She has been harassed, threatened, and abused—and I do not want to see this happen to her, her family, or employees of GSA.[18]" Absolutely not true. The only pressure she faced was to do her job.

Trump goes on to say,

> Our case STRONGLY continues, we will keep up the good fight, and I believe we will prevail! Nevertheless, in the best interest of our Country, I am recommending that Emily and her team do what needs to be done with regard to initial protocols, and have told my team to do the same.

Now that Trump has finally given the go-ahead for the GSA process of "ascertainment," Biden's team can now access government data and make contact with federal agencies and get access to $6.3 million in government funding for the transition. Top of the priority list for the Biden team is gaining access to COVID-19 data and the vaccine distribution plans.

But today, even before Trump's approval that ascertainment protocols proceed, Biden is announcing his nominees for cabinet appointments, which need to be approved by the Senate. He has already announced Janet Yellen as the first female treasury secretary, and today he announced his key national security and foreign policy teams.

It looks like a pretty impressive mix and certainly ticks the diversity box that Biden promised. All of these individuals are known personally to Biden. *The Guardian* has provided a brief biography on each nominee, which is worth a quick look if only for the record.

---

[18] The GSA assists with presidential transition, providing support to the president-elect and vice president-elect, inter-agency transition, presidential inauguration, and the outgoing president and vice president. Upon request, it provides services and facilities to each eligible candidate for use in preparing to assume their official duties.

Janet Yellen—Treasury Secretary

A seventy-four-year-old economist was the first woman to chair the US Federal Reserve and looks set to achieve another first: becoming the country's first female treasury secretary. Yellen is an expert in labour markets and has highlighted the economic impact of uneven growth in the jobs market. Donald Trump declined to reappoint her after his election, making her the first central bank chief not to serve two terms since the Carter administration.

Anthony Blinken—Secretary of State

He is a former deputy secretary of state and a committed internationalist, who spent some of his childhood in Paris and is fluent in French. He views US engagement with the world, and particularly Europe, as vital. He was a member of Bill Clinton's White House staff in the 1990s and served under President Barack Obama. He's not a fan of Brexit and described it last year as "a total mess."

Alejandro Mayorkas—Secretary of Homeland Security

Described by the former Democratic presidential candidate Julián Castro as "a historic and experienced choice to lead an agency in desperate need of reform," the Cuban American lawyer served as the deputy secretary of homeland security for nearly three years under Obama. Formerly Obama's director of US citizenship and immigration services, if confirmed, the sixty-one-year-old would be the first Latino and the first immigrant to lead the department.

Linda Thomas-Greenfield—US Ambassador to the United Nations

An African American native of Louisiana, Thomas-Greenfield was formerly assistant secretary of state for African affairs under the Obama and Trump administrations. She was also the US ambassador to Liberia under George W. Bush and Obama. Of her appointment, Thomas-Greenfield, sixty-eight, has said, "My mother taught me to lead with the power of kindness and compassion to make the world a better place. I've carried that lesson with me throughout my career in foreign service and, if confirmed, will do the same as ambassador to the United Nations."

John Kerry—Special Presidential Envoy for Climate

Well-known internationally, Kerry will take the lead on combating the climate crisis. The seventy-six-year-old lost the 2004 US election to George W. Bush before going on to become secretary of state from 2013 to 2017 under Obama. His position as special presidential envoy for climate is new and will not need to approved by the Senate.

Avril Haines—Director of National Intelligence

A New York-born lawyer, she was previously deputy director of the CIA, the first woman to hold that position. She worked closely with Biden from 2007 to 2008 in her role as deputy chief counsel for the Senate Democrats. Haines, fifty-one, was also the first female deputy national security adviser and, if confirmed, will become the first woman to be the director of national intelligence.

Jake Sullivan—National Security Adviser

Sullivan was the national security adviser to Biden when he was vice president and served as deputy chief of staff to Hillary Clinton when she was secretary of state. Since 2014, Sullivan, forty-three, has been teaching at Yale Law School.

The Dow Jones Breaks through 30,000

When the Dow crashed from its 29,500 high back in February, I said Trump would never see that figure again. I also expected the

Dow to fall if it looked like Biden was going to win the election as would typically be the case ahead of an anticipated Democratic victory. Wrong! Today, 24 November, the Dow broke through the magical 30,000-point barrier; and Biden's determination to get the pandemic under control and the prospects that brings with it have a lot to do with that.

I didn't mention that the lowest point the Dow reached this year was on 23 March when it was 18,600, nearly 11,000 points down from its high, so to break through 30,000 is amazing.

Trump has been virtually invisible since he lost the election, but he suddenly sprang to life and called reporters to the White House briefing room to mark this landmark breakthrough. It was bizarre. He came in with Pence, spoke for a mere sixty seconds, then left.

He referred to the positive news over the last three weeks with the announcements of promising COVID-19 vaccines from Pfizer, Moderna, and Oxford-AstraZeneca. He said, "I'm very thrilled with what's happened on the vaccine front. That's been absolutely incredible. Nothing like that has ever happened medically, and I think people are acknowledging that. And it's having a big effect."

He could not resist the temptation to make himself part of the success. He also said, "The stock market's just broken 30,000. Never been broken, that number. That's a sacred number. Nobody thought they'd ever see it. That's the ninth time since the beginning of 2020, and it's the forty-eighth time that we've broken records during the Trump administration."

He went on to congratulate all the people in the administration "who have worked so hard" and finished by saying, "And most importantly, I want to congratulate the people of our country because there are no people like you." Very touching, but the whole event reeked of being staged for posterity.

Trump Pardons Flynn

Today, 25 November, we wake to the news that Trump has pardoned Lieutenant General Michael Flynn, former national security adviser in the Trump administration, who had pleaded guilty to a felony count of "willfully and knowingly" making false statements to the FBI and agreed to cooperate with Special Counsel Robert Mueller's investigation into Russia's interference into the 2016 election.

Flynn had resigned from his position after it was discovered that he had misled Mike Pence about the nature and content of his communications with Sergey Kislyak, Russian ambassador to the US. He held the position for only twenty-four days.

Flynn also served in the Obama administration as director of the Defence Intelligence Agency from July 2012 to August 2014, when he was fired. Obama warned Trump against taking on Flynn. More pardons are reportedly under consideration, so we can be sure there will be more to say on this in the weeks ahead.

All presidents issue pardons before they leave office, and some pardons make you raise your eyebrows. Bill Clinton, for example, pardoned his half-brother Roger Clinton for drug charges even though he had served his sentence more than a decade earlier.

More controversially, on his last day in office, 20 January 2001, Clinton pardoned Marc Rich, an international trader and friend who fled to Switzerland during his prosecution owing $48 million in taxes.

However, what makes the Flynn pardon especially interesting is that Flynn originally promised to cooperate with the Mueller investigation (which may not have been good for Trump), but he later became more combative, coincidentally after Trump dangled the prospect of a pardon under his nose.

Flynn then changed his legal team and accused the Justice Department of entrapment and moved to withdraw his guilty plea. The Justice Department, at the instruction of none other Attorney General William Barr—Trump-sycophant extraordinaire—later moved to drop its case against Flynn, prompting the resignation of one of the prosecutors in disgust.

This is new territory. The AG has always been independent. But under Trump, you are loyal to him, or you're out. So now, with Flynn pardoned, he can't be further investigated and so won't say anything to incriminate Trump.

But having been pardoned, Flynn can no longer invoke the Fifth Amendment's protection against self-incrimination, which could be problematic if he is called to testify before a jury in the future. If he refuses to testify, he would risk being charged with contempt of court.

Trump Keeps on Whining

Trump was due to be in Pennsylvania today attending a meeting of state senators at a Gettysburg hotel but cancelled because yet another White House aide was diagnosed with COVID. Instead, he phoned in, saying Pennsylvania's results "should be overturned" because he actually won "by a lot." Actually, he lost by a lot—170,000 votes to be precise.

He said the election was rigged, that they cheated and that it was fraudulent. In other words, the same unsubstantiated charges were trotted out for the umpteenth time. And remember, despite making these charges publicly, they have never been made in front of any judge in the thirty-plus lawsuits either dropped or lost—nor have any of Trump's advocates provided any evidence to back up their claims.

Trump's whining knows no end. If the Democrats had tried to rig the election, they did a pretty shitty job. For a start, proper rigging would have ensured a better result with House seats. As it was, although holding onto the majority, Democrats lost a net twelve seats.

Rather than losing seats, they would have gained more. They also totally messed up with the Senate. Instead of having a comfortable majority, we now await Georgia!

Trump Team Sends Hundreds of Emails Asking for Money

Capitalising on the disappointment of his supporters, Trump's campaign team has been sending out hundreds of emails—well over three hundred so far (by mid-December, this number increases beyond four hundred)—asking supporters for contributions of $5 to $45 for his election defence fund.

One email from Tweedledumb reads, "The Left will try to STEAL this Election!"; and Pence warns that "the stakes have never been higher, which is why I'm coming to you with an urgent request."

And more disturbingly from Team Trump 2020:

> This is your FINAL NOTICE. So far, you've ignored all our emails asking you to join us in DEFENDING THE ELECTION. You've ignored Team Trump, Eric, Lara, Don, the Vice-President AND you've even ignored the President of the United States. TENS OF THOUSANDS of Patriots have stepped up for the VERY FIRST TIME in the last 48 hours—why haven't you?

But all is not as it seems. The fine print of these donation requests, ostensibly to cover the legal fees of court cases to defend the Trump's fight against the election results, can also be used to repay campaign debt, replenish the Republican National Committee, and to help establish Trump's new political action committee (PAC), Save America. In other words, more money for One-Term to play with.

This PAC can accept donations of up to $5,000 per donor per year from an unlimited number of donors. It can also accept donations from other PACs, the majority of which Trump can use to help fund other candidates; pay for staff; and pay travel expenses, personal expenses, and even consultancy fees!

It smells like a slush fund, and it looks totally like Trump is conning his supporters. Raising funds for one purpose and using them for another is known in some jurisdictions as raising money under false pretences, but I doubt his base would care.

I said just over a week ago that Trump was losing it mentally, but I think he knew exactly what he was doing. It's all about the money.

Oh yes, Trump can also use the funds to finance another shot at the presidency in 2024, something he is reportedly considering, but I doubt he will run as I can't see him risking the ignominy of losing again.

He'll probably settle for being a kingmaker if he can't be king. It will all depend on how much more he can con those who unbelievably still support him.

We already know the only person Trump cares for is himself. His ego is so big there is no room in his world for anyone else. He needs to be relevant, and he craves the limelight. But living the life of a one-term former president gives him neither.

However, he does understand power and knows how to use it, and his Save America PAC should give him the funds to hold sway over Republicans so that they exist only by virtue of his grace and favour.

He's tasted what it is to be "the most powerful man in the world" and wants to continue feasting. It will be interesting to see how this plays out.

However, what might be good for One-Term will absolutely not work out well in the long term for the Republican Party. They need to be shot of him—and the sooner the better. Not an easy task.

Thanksgiving Day 2020

This is an important day in the calendar for Americans, falling on the fourth Thursday of November. It's traditionally a day when families get together around the dinner table and give thanks to God for the good things in their lives.

Even for those who are not religious, giving thanks is a common practice. It's a good tradition to have, if only because when you take time to appreciate what you have yourself, it gives you pause to think about those less fortunate.

However, this year, with coronavirus cases now through thirteen million, breaking records nearly every day; hospitalisations at a record ninety-three thousand; and deaths of over 263,000, a lot of families are struggling to know what to give thanks for.

The number of people travelling in the lead-up to Thanksgiving Day exceeded the worst fears of medical experts and the CDC, who warned against family gatherings over the holiday period.

Family gatherings have reportedly been one of the major spreading events of coronavirus. An estimated three million travellers passed through US airports in the days leading up to the holiday, and they still have to fly back. A further spike in coronavirus cases seems inevitable in the coming weeks.

Despite hospitals being at or near capacity, the issue is now less a case of bed space availability but more a lack of medical staff to care for the sick.

Hospitalisations are expected to continue to rise, but many states are concerned that their ability to care for patients will be compromised. To make matters worse, Christmas is just around the corner.

Justice Amy Coney Barrett, Please Show Yourself

I wrote how the religion of the right might shape the country following Amy Barrett's appointment to the Supreme Court, but I didn't expect to see evidence of it quite so soon.

A few weeks ago, New York state's governor, Cuomo, imposed a limit on the number of people gathering in places of worship because numbers were growing in churches and synagogues, particularly in Brooklyn, where the virus had spiked.

Cuomo had established "orange zones" and "red zones," designated according to local positivity rates. His decision was challenged in court but was upheld. It was appealed to the Supreme Court where the nine justices found five to four in favour of the churches and synagogues, with Barrett's vote being decisive.

What was surprising about this was that both Nevada and California had similar cases earlier in the year; but on those occasions, the justices went the other way, again five to four, upholding the lower courts' decisions.

Barrett's arrival on the scene, replacing Bader Ginsberg, has therefore had a pretty immediate impact.

After Supreme Court decisions are made, justices' opinions are published, and it was clear there was strong disagreement between the justices in this case.

Responding to other opinions, Justice Sonia Sotomayor, joined by Justice Elena Kagan, were clearly not impressed with the majority decision, writing, "Justices of this court play a deadly game in second-guessing the expert judgment of health officials about the environments in which a contagious virus, now infecting a million Americans each week, spreads most easily."

Calls are already being heard among Democrats for the new Biden administration to increase the number of justices to "restore the balance"—but he'll need the Senate to do that.

Anyway, I'm not sure that's the solution; but the current structure of justices, being lifetime appointments, is completely outdated. It would make sense to set an age limit with reelections, say, every seven to ten years. No matter what, changes need to be made.

However, all may not be doom and gloom. The justices will need to pick their battles carefully as if they systematically draw a red line through all Democrat-supported cases, there will very likely be repercussions when the moment allows.

Trump Answers Journalists' Questions

For the first time since he lost the election, Trump appeared in front of journalists on 25 November to answer questions. Frankly, he needn't have bothered. It was more of his "It's all a fraud," "It was rigged" story line; and it's becoming tiresome listening to him.

Reuters White House correspondent Jeff Mason got on the wrong side of Trump while asking him whether he would concede the election to Joe Biden if the Electoral College votes in favor of Biden.

Trump had tried to bluster his way through the question but, when pressed, just lost it. "Don't talk to me that way. You're just a lightweight. Don't talk to me that way. I'm the president of the United States. Don't ever talk to the president that way." What a child!

Trump didn't have much to say about coronavirus, but he did have something to say about the vaccines: "Don't let him [Biden] take credit for the vaccines because the vaccines were me, and I pushed people harder than they've ever been pushed before."

He also had something to say about Brad Raffensperger, Georgia's secretary of state, calling him "an enemy of the people" for certifying the election as a Biden win. The man simply oozes lack of class.

Trump Calls into Fox

Since Fox also called the election for Biden, it has been on Trump's shit list. Yesterday, in advance of his appearance, by phone, he tweeted that Fox News was "virtually unwatchable, especially during the weekend," and urged people to watch Newsmax TV, a hitherto little-known super-right-wing channel, saying all the things election-deniers want to hear.

Since Trump first touted Newsmax, Fox viewers have reportedly "flocked" there to soak up its rhetoric.

Irrespective of what I think about Fox, Trump's reaction to their calling the election for Biden is pathetic. Fox has been Trump's strongest mainstream-media supporter, promulgating all his lies and BS, but in a heartbeat, he drops them. This shows just how shallow and artificial he is as if we didn't already know.

Sunday's interview with Fox's Maria Bartiromo was Trump's first since losing the election. It was less of an interview but more of a forty-five-minute monologue, but again, Trump had nothing of substance to say. It was "same old, same old" as he rambled on with one accusation after another, alleging fraud without substantiating anything, and was barely challenged by Bartiromo.

He expressed his frustration at almost everybody but had some special words for Georgia's governor Brian Kemp, who, despite being a Trump supporter, has refused to denounce the election result, saying, "The governor has done nothing [to overturn the election]. He's done absolutely nothing. I'm ashamed that I endorsed him. But I look at what's going on—it's so terrible." Trump was simply frustrated that Kemp wasn't corrupt.

Apart from being another Trump rant, it was hard to find anything from what he said in the interview that was truthful. Yashar Ali, who contributes to *New York Magazine* and *HuffPost*, tweeted that the interview was "filled with so many lies and so much misinformation, probably more than any interview during his presidency."

It's tempting to quote a list of the lies he spouted, but I can't be bothered. But I will mention that while he accepts he got seventy-four million votes, he cannot accept Biden got eighty million!

Trump said, "We won the election easily. There's no way Joe Biden got eighty million votes." If it wasn't true, it would be unbelievable! This man really does live in a world of his own.

I'm reminded of when Tosser Ted Cruz was running for president in 2015. He accused Trump of being "utterly amoral" and "a narcissist at a level I don't think this country's ever seen."

He also said Trump was "a pathological liar," adding, "He doesn't know the difference between truth and lies. He lies [with] practically every word that comes out of his mouth."

Cruz was right, but he's changed his mind since then, not because he likes his orange friend. It's simply political expedience being exercised by a man with higher political ambition, who doesn't realise he has no hope.

De Blasio Backtracks on School Closures in New York City

Still on Sunday, Mayor Bill de Blasio announces he will reopen public elementary schools. This is in response to widespread criticism from parents and others. De Blasio said that middle and high schools will remain closed but children in prekindergarten and elementary school can return starting 7 December. He also said he will review how schools are managed during the pandemic and that he will abandon the 3 percent positivity test threshold. It makes sense.

December 2020

2 December: Britain Approves the Pfizer Vaccine

Today, Britain gives emergency authorisation to Pfizer/BioNTech's coronavirus vaccine, becoming the first Western country to do so. Vaccinations, which have proven 95 percent successful in trials, will reportedly start as early as next week, beginning with the elderly in care homes and care-home staff.

It is anticipated that everyone in the UK, with its population of sixty million, will be vaccinated by the end of the spring. This is a massive relief and gives real hope everywhere that the beginning of the end is in sight.

Things are a little different in the US as we await the soon-expected FDA approval, but even so, the sense of relief is palpable. Of course, with a population five times more than that of the UK, vaccinating the whole country is a totally different prospect, but there is also the issue of trust.

Currently, only 42 percent of Americans say they will have the vaccine, and whilst that is very low, I expect the percentage to improve as the vaccine rolls out and its efficacy can be seen in the clear light of day instead of through the fog of partisanship. I hope I'm proved right.

New Records Set in the US

One day after the welcome vaccination news, we are given a harsh reminder that we're a long way from putting the coronavirus behind us. Today, as total cases break through fourteen million, the daily tally of new cases exceeds two hundred thousand for the first time. Hospitalisations top one hundred thousand, and deaths hit a record for a single day of 2,800. This is a living nightmare.

But to make things worse, we have yet to see the expected impact of Thanksgiving celebrations. Hospitals are at bursting point, and medical teams are at breaking point.

If we don't change our behaviour, some of the projections are frightening, showing cases at three hundred thousand a day with hospitalisations potentially doubling and deaths hitting 3,000 and more a day. Being at those levels is unthinkable.

Europe is also struggling with the winter surge, but that doesn't mean things couldn't have been better here. Looking back to when this started, I wrote of Trump being asked in January if he thought COVID would become a pandemic.

He said not. He said it was "totally under control. It's going to be just fine." Only six weeks later, not only had he changed his mind, but he had changed his truth, famously saying, "This is a pandemic. I felt it was a pandemic long before it was called a pandemic."

It is so disheartening to be in this position, but as dire as things are, Trump still says nothing—absolutely nothing! It is utterly shameful. We never got "close to zero." The virus didn't "disappear," and there was no "miracle."

With all that's happening today, the only thing Trump cares about is poisoning the validity of the election. Tragic.

Will Bill Barr Be Barred?

Successor to fired Jeff Sessions, Attorney General Bill Barr, one of Trump's most loyal lapdogs, may well soon find that his basket has been moved to another room. Bad dog! Barr has supported Trump at every turn; he's always been there for him. He even stepped in to lend his considerable weight to support Fat Boy over his mail-in ballots bollocks.

But Barr may no longer be one particular man's best friend! In an interview with the *AP*, Barr said that US attorneys and FBI agents have been working to follow up on complaints and information they've received about voting, saying, "To date, we have not seen fraud on a scale that could have effected a different outcome in the election." Whoops!

Trump was not a happy chappy. Barr initiated the inquiry in early November without any evidence of voting irregularities. At the time, I wrote of Barr acting as Trump's personal attorney, so I was surprised that he also said in the *AP* interview, "There's a growing tendency to use the criminal justice system as sort of a default fix-all, and people don't like something they want the Department of Justice to come in and investigate." Sounds a bit like a dig at the Porky One to me.

As a result of all this, Barr met with Trump at the White House recently. The meeting was said to have been contentious and that Trump "erupted" at what Barr had said; so the question is, "Will Trump fire him?" But the question I have is, "Does anyone care?"

There is currently a discussion going on among pundits whether Barr has finally had enough and decided to speak the truth. It doesn't matter! His tenure as AG expires as soon as Biden is sworn in, so I don't see anything noble in his actions.

If anything, it's a cynical move to present himself as a man of principles instead of a weaseling, arse-kissing sycophant. He probably wants to be fired; I'm sure he thinks that would be even better for his legacy.

Georgia's on Everybody's Mind

Trump still will not let go of the election result in Georgia. Biden's winning margin was a narrow fourteen thousand votes, and a recount was ordered by Secretary of State Brad Raffensperger.

The recount confirmed Biden's win but with a reduced majority of twelve thousand. Still unhappy, the Trump team called for another recount while in the meantime, Trump was referring to the Georgia election as a joke with more false claims about fraudulent votes.

At the beginning of this mess, Raffensperger was called by none other than Loser Lindsey to see if he thought poll workers may have been politically biased when looking at ballots with non-matching signatures and if he had the authority to discard certain mail-in ballots.

According to *USA Today*, it appeared to Raffensperger that Graham was suggesting he find a method to throw out ballots that had been lawfully cast as Raffensperger said, "It sure looked like he was wanting to go down that road."

Raffensperger said in a radio interview, "They say that as pressure builds, it reveals your character. It doesn't change your character. Some people aren't behaving too well with seeing where the results are."

By the way, Loser Lindsey also called election officials in Nevada and Arizona with the same questions. Naturally, Lindsey was calling only to find out how the process works in those states!

At a press conference, one of Raffensperger's senior deputies, Gabriel Sterling, demonstrated his frustration and concerns at the constant stream of contumely and accusations, saying, "Mr. President, it looks like you likely lost the state of Georgia. We're investigating. There's always a possibility. I get it. You have the right to go to the courts."

But he then added, "What you don't have is the ability to— and you need to step up and say this—stop inspiring people to commit potential acts of violence. Someone's going to get hurt. Someone's going to get shot. Someone's going to get killed." Prophetic words?

He finished by including the two senators who have been absent in their condemnation ahead of January's runoff Senate election. "Mr. President, you have not condemned these actions or this language. Senators, you have not condemned this language or these actions. This has to stop. We need you to step up."

The next day, Raffensperger called on Trump to stop with his allegations of fraudulent votes being cast. He even cited the newly reformed AG Bill Barr, saying, "President Trump's Justice Department has seen no widespread fraud. They have had multiple investigations like us. And our investigators have seen no wide-spread fraud, either."

Emotions are so high that Raffensperger and Governor Brian Kemp, a new Trump target, are protected by security details. But what was Trump's reaction to these comments? Well, he tweeted, "Expose the massive voter fraud in Georgia." Another example of real class!

But the madness doesn't end there. Trump supporters held a rally in a park about twenty-five miles north of Atlanta, where they fantasised about overturning the election. They booed at the mention of Governor Kemp's name, chanting "lock him up," and there were calls for others to be held to account for not doing enough to help Trump substantiate his bogus election claims.

This is like an internecine war, and all this nonsense does nothing to help the two Senate candidates in their January runoff elections.

A couple of weeks ago, I warned that Republicans may not vote in January's runoff election if they believed the fix was in. Amazingly, at the rally, some radicals even called for Republicans to boycott the elections.

Should they lose, there is no doubt that Trump will have played a major part. But none of this worries Trump; he continues unabashed with his lies and accusations. And ahead of a rally in Georgia, he called Governor Kemp of Georgia and asked him to overturn the election result!

Unfortunately for Trump, under Georgia law, the only person who can overturn an election is the secretary of state, one Brad "Enemy of the People" Raffensperger—so good luck.

Truth and facts are irrelevant to Trump. What matters to him is what he can get people to believe, and he is being successful. Huge swathes of his supporters are passionately loyal and swallow everything he says hook, line, and sinker. Trump is clearly aware of the first rule of propaganda: "If you tell a lie big enough and keep repeating it, people will eventually come to believe it."

Trump Holds Rally in Georgia

On Saturday, 5 December, Trump's rally in Georgia is ostensibly to mobilise Republicans to vote for the two Republican senators, Kelly Loeffler and David Perdue, in the upcoming runoff election.

The first thing to note is that no one behind Trump is wearing a mask, unlike at his pre-election rallies where masks were compulsory for those behind him. It's always about the optics.

While he did urge supporters to vote for Loeffler and Perdue, his entreaties did not ring true. In fact, he sounded exactly like the hypocrite he is as he again beat the drum of division, saying, "If you don't vote, the socialists and the communists—they win."

In other words, when you voted before, we lost because it was crooked, but you should vote again because we need to win.

He showed a number of clips from right-wing TV channels, each fully supporting his ridiculous claims. It was pure narcissism, but it also served to reinforce his message to the faithful.

It was as if he was saying, "Look, it's not just me. Others are saying I won as well." It also shows what television he watches when he's not playing golf.

Vaccinations Are Here!

What a great day, 8 December 2020! We learn today that in the UK, the first person to be vaccinated against COVID-19 with the Pfizer/BioNTech vaccine is a ninety-year-old lady by the name of Margaret Keenan. She is fabulous and defies her ninety years and was fully supportive of everyone following her lead.

The first man to receive the vaccine in the UK is none other than a certain William Shakespeare! I can imagine the nurse's dilemma: "To vaccinate or not to vaccinate, that is the question."

This is indeed a great day, but it goes without saying we are a long way from returning to a life that is even remotely normal. But these vaccinations show us that we have at least taken the first steps in that direction.

Supreme Court Kicks Out Plea to Overturn Pennsylvania Election Result

The Supreme Court rejected a lawsuit brought by Pennsylvanian Republicans, which argued that a 2019 state law authorising mail-in voting is unconstitutional and that all mail-in ballots cast in the Pennsylvania election should be thrown out. The Supreme Court dealt with the case in one line: "The application for injunctive relief presented to Justice Alito and by him referred to the Court is denied."

Frankly, this whole story stinks. Prior to the case being appealed to the Supreme Court, it had been unanimously rejected by the justices of Pennsylvania's own Supreme Court on the grounds that the petitioners had waived their opportunity to challenge before the election but chose instead to "lay by and gamble upon receiving a favorable decision of the electorate."

Justice Wecht went on to say, "It is not our role to lend legitimacy to such transparent and untimely efforts to subvert the will of Pennsylvania voters."

But The Fight Goes On in Texas

You would think these defeats would bring a crashing end to this nonsense, but no. After Pennsylvania, Trump still wants to fight on. He tweeted, "We will be INTERVENING in the Texas (plus many other states) case. This is the big one. Our Country needs a victory!"

He's supporting Texas attorney general Ken Paxton's crazy efforts to sue Georgia, Michigan, Pennsylvania, and Wisconsin, claiming they broke the law when they made changes to election procedures due to the pandemic.

This translates into his asking the Supreme Court—with the signatures of another seventeen attorneys general and 126 Republican House members—to overturn Trump's defeat, thereby negating more than ten million Democratic votes. Yes, he really is doing that! Yes, he really is that crazy!

Fortunately, the Supreme Court was to throw out the case, saying in part, "Texas has not demonstrated a judiciary cognizable interest in the manner in which another state conducts its elections."

But as is so often in these mad times, things may not quite be as they seem. It turns out that since 2015, Crazy Ken has been under indictment for securities fraud charges, and just a few weeks ago, seven of his top aides accused him of using his office to serve the interests of a political donor. According to the *Associated Press*, the FBI is investigating these claims.

As we are nearing the pardon season, perhaps Paxton is hoping Trump will hand one out to him.

What makes this so sad is that Trump is walking all over the Constitution, and Republicans are not only allowing him to do it, but they're supporting him. This is a disgusting and shameful disregard of the democratic process and for all norms of decency.

They all swear an oath to the Constitution. They all pray to God, and they're all full of shit.

Who Are Trump's Voters?

Right! I've had enough writing about Trump's post-election shenanigans, so it's time to change the tempo. And what better way to do that than to try to work out who votes for this madman and why they do it.

I have a longtime Republican friend, CW, who voted for Trump but admits Trump is flawed, even seriously flawed. He voted for him in 2016 and 2020 because despite the man, he "likes his policies." CW correctly sees me as anti-Trump. I cannot stand the man, Trump, that is; and I disliked and distrusted him long before he entered politics.

Let's face it. He is a serial failure as a businessman. He has no leadership skills and has absolutely no relationship with the truth. He deliberately divided the country in the hope of achieving a second term, believing his base would pull him through.

But who makes up his base? Just as there are ever-Democrats, there are ever-Republicans, many of whom are found among non-college-educated Whites. And it is they who make up a good slice of the foundation.

Add to them those Democrats who, in 2016, would not vote for Hillary under any circumstances. Next, take a sprinkling of voters who liked the idea of someone with a completely different approach, and top with a healthy serving of those who lapped up Trump's xenophobic rhetoric. And for good measure, I will offer up a side dish of right-wing extremists.

Simply put, I think that was Trump's 2016 base, but I believe his 2020 base is slightly different as the Democrats probably won back the never-Hillary voters. And Trump expanded his right-wing followers—idiot groups like QAnon, Proud Boys, other conspiracy theorists, neo-Nazis, and fascist groups.

But there is another group that became increasingly important to Trump: Latino men. In general, they perceive Trump as having a macho no-nonsense approach, and they see Biden as weak.

Trump is particularly strong in Florida, where his anti-communism position resonates well with Cubans and Venezuelans. He's also expanded his appeal among Latino evangelicals throughout the country. So even though he lost some suburban women voters, his base has become more diverse.

But I cannot fully understand how anybody could have voted for Trump this time. I suspect a good chunk of his base feel that with Trump, they have someone who actually listens to them and cares for them. He may listen, but he certainly doesn't care.

CW worked internationally for many years and understands how to work with people from different cultures. He has a good view of the world, yet he voted for Trump both times. Why? He's not stupid.

Despite reservations he had about Trump personally, he tells me he was still able to look through the man, to his policies. But CW is not only a Republican. He is also strongly against many of the Democrat's policies, having written,

> We particularly don't appreciate an ever-grow-
> ing, and ever-more-expensive, Washington
> DC bureaucracy farming out taxpayer dollars
> to stagnant and nonproductive social programs
> that produce not one iota of tangible reward.
> Take all the "clean air" subsidies that have been
> given to "climate control" proponents, billions
> of US taxpayers dollars spent, and yet, electric-
> ity rates keep going up year after year…some-
> thing is rotten in paradise, and Trump identi-
> fied that "rot"!

So maybe it's the combination of supporting Trump's Republican policies and not liking Democrat policies that still makes CW a Trump voter. It could also be that he's simply a dyed-in-the-wool Republican, who is able to ignore the tweets, ignore the lies, and ignore the now forty failed court cases aimed at overturning the election.

Or maybe, he just doesn't want a Democrat in the White House under any circumstances! I say that because CW also writes,

> The one thing that stands out this year is that
> otherwise perfectly rational people have devel-
> oped such a visceral hatred of Trump that they
> blindly rush into grasp any wisp of disaccord
> in what Trump does and labels it seditious?
> And, of course, the left-wing media jumps in
> as a Greek chorus! Russian collusion, my foot!
> It turned out to be a plain and simple FBI-led
> attempted coup-d'état of a sitting President.
> But it is this visceral "hate" of Trump that ulti-
> mately did him in.

Not sure I agree there. I have no doubt that visceral hatred contributed to Trump's fall, but ultimately, he was the architect of his own demise.

However, I am encouraged that CW also told me that should Trump stand again, he would be a "much harder taskmaster" in deciding whether to vote for him, which is reassuring. Also, he is broadly accepting of Biden's early personnel selections and believes "Biden is entitled to one hundred days of peace and quiet to start doing what he's going to do."

It's likely that CW and I will always struggle to find common ground when it comes to Trump, but whilst I am definitely a never-Trumper, I am not a never-Republican. But the qualities of a leader of any party matter to me.

A leader does not have to be perfect but should have an appreciation of what the position means, a willingness to listen, the ability to attract the right people into critical positions, openness, and transparency; but Trump is devoid of all these qualities and a whole load more besides.

True, he made some good appointments, but they never lasted long because Trump always knew best.

Neither am I an avowed Biden supporter, but Trump is out, which is a massive positive for me. I fully agree with CW that Biden should be allowed to get on with things for the first one hundred days, but thereafter, he's fair game.

I am glad Biden is not out there on the left. I have little time for extremes of any type, and I believe Biden is what is needed at the moment. The task ahead of him is monumental, exacerbated by Trump's ridiculous behaviour, but I firmly believe if he has any success in addressing the widening wealth gap, he may just win over some of Trump's base.

As I have said many times, one of Trump's major failings is he has no understanding of what it takes to be a president. He always makes it about him. He can't even understand how other Republicans managed to get reelected when he didn't. He doesn't get that this was not a Republican/Democrat election—it was a referendum on him.

He governed for his own benefit, aided and abetted by his self-serving family, and he lost. I am staggered that even today, people support and defend him and that seventy-two million people voted for him in 2020. Clearly, I have a lot to learn.

Trump demanded loyalty to him rather than to the Constitution. He had, and still has, such a grip over the Republican Party that there are few Republicans prepared to say anything against him, let alone acknowledge Biden as president-elect. You cross DT at your peril.

The First Vaccinations in the US

Today, Monday, 14 December, is historic as the first Americans receive their coronavirus vaccines. The speed at which the vaccine has been developed, tested, and approved exceeds even the most optimistic of expectations. There is justifiably a great sense of achievement and hope.

The Electoral College Casts Its Votes

This event always takes place on the first Monday after the second Wednesday in December.

Normally, when the Electoral College casts its votes for president and vice president, the day passes without much notice as it is more of a formality; but today, given Trump's continuing refusal to concede, it is seen by some as confirmation of Biden's win—again!

By the way, Biden does win. He wins by 306 to 232. Oh, and by the way, Trump says Biden didn't win. Oh, and by the way, Trump is talking bollocks.

When Trump was campaigning in 2016, he declared, "We're going to win so much you're going to be so sick and tired of winning." I should think by now, it's Biden who is sick and tired of winning as he's won this election countless times at this point.

After casting their votes, the electors sign six "Certificates of the Vote," which are delivered to various people, the most important of whom is the president of the Senate—namely, VP Mike Pence. These certificates must be delivered by the fourth

Wednesday in December, which this year is 23 December. At that point, the electors' job is done.

So What Happens Next?

Responsibility for electing the president then falls to Congress, which will meet on 6 January 2021 at 1:00 p.m. The Senate and House of Representatives will meet in a joint session to count the electors' votes and declare the winners. Finally, on 20 January 2021, the president and vice president named by Congress will be inaugurated—at last marking the end to a long and grueling election season.

Big Bad Bill Barr Bails

Barr resigns, but his resignation letter is pathetic. It could have been written by Trump himself. In fact, it probably was as it lists one "success" after another. Barr writes to Trump, saying, "I am proud to have played a role in the many successes and unprecedented achievements you have delivered for the American people. Your record is all the more historic because you accomplished it in the face of relentless, implacable resistance." Yuck!

He then continues to massage Trump's ego, saying, "Your 2016 victory speech in which you reached out to your opponents and called for working together for the benefit of the American people was immediately met by a partisan onslaught against you in which no tactic, no matter how abusive and deceitful, was out of bounds. The nadir of this campaign was the effort to cripple, if not oust, your administration with frenzied and baseless accusations of collusion with Russia."

He adds, "You built the strongest and most resilient economy in American history," and best of all, "By brokering historic peace deals in the Mideast, you have achieved what most thought impossible." Whaaat?

This has "Trump" written all over it. But no matter, he's gone—and that does matter.

One More Thing about Today

Coronavirus deaths in the US pass three hundred thousand individuals. I don't know what to say.

McConnell Finally Acknowledges Biden as President-Elect

On 15 December, six weeks after the election, Senate majority leader Mitch McConnell finally congratulates Joe Biden and Kamala Harris on their election victory, formally recognising them as president-elect and vice president-elect, respectively, for the first time. This comes one day after the Electoral College cast its votes.

He also recognised Kamala Harris's achievement, saying, "All Americans can take pride that our nation has a female vice president-elect for the first time."

Sad that he had to wait so long before doing the right thing. Actually, it's pathetic.

OK, How about Martial Law?

The newly pardoned retired Lieutenant General Michael Flynn has got a great idea. With Trump now having failed with more than fifty court cases brought by his team or supporters, Mick the Dick, with all his military experience, has come up with the perfect solution—invoke martial law in swing states won by Joe Biden. There you go!

In a 17 December appearance on Trump's new favourite TV station, Newsmax, Flynn said of the swing states that Trump could "take military capabilities and basically rerun an election in each of those states." WTF? He's already disgraced himself as Trump's National Security advisor, and now he's disgracing the uniform he once wore. This whacko is as certifiable as Trump!

There is no chance that Trump will (be allowed to) invoke martial law, but what is disturbing is how much traction the story got, so much so that Army secretary Ryan McConnell and Army chief of staff general James McConville felt compelled to issue a joint statement, saying, "There is no role for the US military in determining the outcome of an American election."

What Trump is doing is so destructive to the country, but he doesn't care. He's like one of his fellow one-termers, Herbert Hoover, who created so much turmoil prior to Franklyn D Roosevelt taking over back in 1932 that the "lame duck" period[19] was shortened from 4 March to 20 January. Perhaps it should be shortened again.

COVID Relief Bill Passed

Late on Monday, 21 December, and after much negotiation, Congress passed a $900 billion relief package that provides a combination of help to individuals and businesses and funds to fight coronavirus. The next day, it was passed by the Senate ninety-two to six, so a good bipartisan result.

AP reports the bill establishes a temporary $300-a-week supplemental jobless benefit and a $600 direct stimulus payment to most Americans. Funds also include a new round of subsidies for hard-hit businesses, restaurants, and theatres and money for schools, healthcare providers, and those facing eviction from rented accommodation.

But having said nothing and done nothing for weeks, Trump is now calling the bill a "disgrace," saying Congress should increase the $600 stimulus payment to $2,000; and he refuses to sign it. Why does he always have to be the centre of attention?

It looks like he is flexing his withering presidential muscles just because he can. He manages to combine being petulant and pathetic at the same time. Maybe his behaviour can give rise to a new word: *pathetulant*, being someone behaving like a spoilt brat when trying to look relevant.

Anyway, our pathetulant signs the bill five days after receiving it but makes no request for any changes other than saying he

---

[19] The approximately ten-week period between election date and the inauguration date.

has secured a commitment from the Senate to consider raising the $600 payment to $2,000. Of course, the Democrats are fully supportive, but for the most part, Republicans are not as they have new-found concerns about the deficit!

So instead of putting forward a stand-alone bill to the Senate for the $2,000 payment, Mitch McConnell adds a couple of poison pills to ensure the bill's failure. He includes a repeal of part of the Communications Act, which provides protection to the likes of Facebook and Twitter for what is posted on their sites, and the establishment of a commission to study voter fraud.

The result? The bill goes forward with the $600 payment as originally approved.

Pardon Season in Full Swing

Having taken a couple of practice swings with a few pardons and commutations, Trump has now really got his eye in. Just before Christmas, he upgraded Roger Stone's July commutation to a full pardon, adding fifteen pardons on Tuesday and twenty-six more on Wednesday. Starting with Stone, here are some of those who received pardons:

Roger Stone, Trump's longtime friend and adviser, was convicted of lying under oath to lawmakers investigating Russian interference in the 2016 US election. A Washington jury in November 2019 convicted Stone on all seven criminal counts of obstruction of a congressional investigation, five counts of making false statements to Congress, and tampering with a witness. The day before Stone was due to report to prison to begin serving a sentence of three years and four months, Trump commuted his sentence.

Paul Manafort, Trump's former campaign chairman, was found guilty of tax fraud and bank fraud in a jury trial in August 2018. A month later, he pleaded guilty to conspiracy charges related to money laundering, lobbying violations, and witness tampering. Prosecutors said he tried to conceal millions of dollars he was paid as a political consultant for pro-Russian Ukrainian politicians. He was sentenced to seven and a half years in prison and, in May, was released to finish his sentence at home due to the coronavirus pandemic.

George Papadopoulos, a former Trump campaign adviser, was sentenced in September 2018 to fourteen days in prison after pleading guilty in October 2017 to lying to the FBI about his contacts with Russian officials and a Maltese professor who told him the Russians had "dirt" on Clinton.

Three former Republican members of Congress—Duncan Hunter of California, Chris Collins of New York, and Steve Stockman of Texas—each received Trump pardons. Hunter pleaded guilty in 2019 to a charge of misusing campaign funds, which he used to pay for a lavish lifestyle. He was due to begin an eleven-month sentence in January.

Collins is serving a twenty-six-month sentence for making false statements to the FBI and for securities fraud. Stockman was sentenced in 2018 to ten years for fraud and money laundering.

The Blackwater Four—Blackwater is an American private military company founded by Erik Prince, a Trump supporter and brother of education secretary Betsy de Vos. (What a coincidence!) In 2007, a group of its employees opened fire on Iraqi civilians, killing fourteen and injuring seventeen, resulting in four guards being charged and convicted. They are Nicholas Slatten, sentenced to life in prison for first degree murder; Paul Slough, fifteen years for voluntary manslaughter; Evan Liberty, fourteen years; and Dustin Heard, sentenced to twelve years and seven months also for voluntary manslaughter.

Charles Kushner—In 2004, father of idiot son Jared pleaded guilty to sixteen counts of tax evasion, one count of witness tampering and one of lying to the Federal Election Commission. He was released in 2006 after serving two years in prison. But this guy is a real crazy.

The witness tampering case concerned none other than his brother-in-law, husband of his sister, who was cooperating with federal investigators against Kushner. In an act of retaliation, Kushner decided to hire a prostitute he knew (I wonder how he knew her) and sent her to his brother-in-law and arranged for their "session" to be videotaped. He then sent the tape to his sister. What a charmer!

So what we learn from this is that if you are a sleazebag and friend of a fat orange person who's president—no worries!

However, by most presidential standards, Trump's pardons are so far relatively few. Obama holds the modern day record with 1,927 acts of clemency, of which 1,715 were commutations.

The large number of commutations came as a result of his administration's initiative to shorten prison terms for inmates convicted of nonviolent drug crimes.

Trump's pardons are for all sorts of dodgy types, 80 percent of whom are connected personally to him in one way or another. A lot more pardons to come, I suspect.

Does Trump Face Prosecution after Leaving Office?

The short answer is yes, but as the saying goes, it's complicated!

There is no track record of any former president being prosecuted. Even Gerald Ford pardoned Richard Nixon after Watergate to prevent the country from becoming further divided.

There are a number of cases against Trump, but there are two cases currently being pursued in New York—one brought by Manhattan district attorney Cyrus Vance and the other by New York state attorney general Letitia James, which could be problematic for Trump.

Attorney General James's case was born out of Trump's former attorney, Michael Cohen, testifying before Congress in February 2020. He testified that he paid porn actress Stormy Daniels $130,000 for the benefit of "Individual 1"—namely, Dodgy Don.

He also said that Trump attributed higher values to property when trying to raise finance from banks and lower values in his tax returns. In March 2019, James subpoenaed records from Deutsche Bank and Investors Bank.

Following *The New York Times*'s revelations in late September 2020 about Trump's tax returns, James sent another subpoena. This time to The Trump Organization for records related to, among other things, consulting fees of some $26 million over ten years, as well as that fee of $740,000 paid to Ivanka Trump.

The other New York case, brought by District Attorney Vance, started along similar lines to that of AG James in that it began as an investigation into pre-election alleged hush money payments made to Stormy Daniels and Karen McDougall, a former *Playboy* model, which transformed into a criminal investigation into Trump and his businesses.

Whilst Vance will not clarify what he is investigating, court papers reportedly suggest it is possibly insurance or financial fraud and possibly tax fraud. His case began over two years ago but has been held up since October 2019 as Trump fought a subpoena to his accounting firm, which was seeking eight years of Trump's tax returns and financial records.

Trump is also being sued by his niece, Mary Trump, who alleges he and his deceased brother deprived her of interests in her father's estate.

It's unclear how these cases will progress, if at all. Opinions are currently mixed with some saying he should pay for what he's done, if he did it. Not to pursue him would validate his "I'm above the law" behaviour. Others believe that a pardon should be given, if needed, so the rift in the country can begin to heal. Of course, he can always try to pardon himself.

For what it's worth, I would like him to serve whatever the maximum penalty is for any crimes he is found guilty of committing. He deserves nothing less.

Biden has said he will not interfere through the Department of Justice—as is Trump's habit—and while he may pardon Trump for federal offences, he can do nothing about state prosecutions. So it's by no means over.

New Year's Eve

Thank goodness we are about to kick 2020 in the arse and push it out of the door. What a relief that vaccines are here. We can now wish and hope for better things in 2021, but it may not be that simple.

Over the past several days, it's been more of the same with Trump, continuing shamelessly to raise funds for his fight against the election result, but luckily, he buggered off to Mar-a-Lago before Christmas to play golf every day.

He's said nothing to explain why only two million vaccinations have been administered from the twenty million his administration promised. Trump's response? None. But if he were to respond, he would probably say "Which club should I take here, a 4- or a 5-iron?"

But in a surprise move, he returned to DC today for the purpose of joining some crazy Republicans who are planning to reject next week's Electoral College certification of Joe Biden's election when Congress meets.

As already noted, this meeting is ceremonial in nature when the vice president counts the votes cast for the candidates and certifies as winners the next president and vice president. But apparently, there are 140 crackpot House members and a handful of GOP senators, including Tosser Ted, who support the notion of rejecting the certification.

The idea is that if Trump can persuade Pence to reject the count, then somehow everything goes back to square one, allowing Trump to win. Un-bloody-believable!

The fact Pence can't do that doesn't seem to matter; but don't think for a moment that any of these tossers, including Trump, actually believes what they are doing is right or will work. Again, for the participants in this sham, it's all about political expedience and being scared of what Trump will do if they don't back him.

The year ends in typical 2020 fashion as COVID cases breach twenty million and record more than ten thousand deaths in the last three days—that's more than two deaths every minute.

And for good measure, a new variant of the virus, identified in the UK about three months ago, has reached the US. This variant is 70 percent more infectious than the original. That's all we need!

January 2021

Welcome 2021

There is a great sense of relief that 2020 is behind us, but it is clear we have a long way to go in fighting the pandemic and are still far from seeing a world that even remotely resembles what we used to call normal. Even so, starting 2021 is emotionally uplifting and gives us pause to look back on what we have all endured. Frankly, it's been absolutely horrible.

But I am encouraged to believe there is an end in sight, even though it may well be much farther down the road than we would like. Despite all that lies ahead, I am still so happy we have closed the door on 2020.

Vaccines Are the Only Solution

Rates of infection are currently growing exponentially and look likely to continue. Here and in many countries in Europe, particularly the UK, it looks like things are getting out of control.

People seem not to care anymore, particularly the millennials and younger. They see treatments have improved, and they are no longer scared of the virus. So even if they do contract COVID, the chances of a full recovery are statistically high. They seem oblivious to the fact that their behaviour exposes other people to the virus.

The hope was that with the arrival of the vaccines, we would all be prepared to tough it out a little longer, but I fear that was wishful thinking. Instead, people are letting their guard down even more, and we are hearing regularly of large numbers of people gathering together, many without masks.

So taking into account Thanksgiving and Christmas surges and adding New Year revelries to the mix, the immediate prospects are not encouraging, but the situation will be worse still if the new more-contagious variant takes hold here. Suddenly, the future does not look bright.

We need to press the reset button and get back to behaving responsibly. However, I don't see this happening, and for that reason, I see our only real hope lies in us all getting vaccinated.

By all accounts, January looks like being the worst month in all respects, but hopes are for a gradual improvement thereafter. I hope that proves true. My ultimate hope is that a single-dose vaccine is produced soon and that, like the measles vaccine, it provides permanent protection. Hope is a good thing!

Trump Asks Raffensperger to "Find" Votes

In an extraordinary turn of events on Saturday, 3 January, a recording, obtained by *The Washington Post*, of a one-hour telephone call Trump made to Brad Raffensperger, Georgia's secretary of state, is released.

Trump, still trying to overturn the election results, directly asks Raffensperger to find votes, saying, "All I want to do is this. I just want to find 11,780 votes, which is one more than we have. Because we won the state."

Trump tells Raffensperger that "the people of Georgia are angry and the people of the country are angry," adding, "and there's nothing wrong with saying that…you know…um…that you've recalculated." Raffensperger simply replies that the data Trump has are wrong.

In a further effort to pressure Raffensperger, Trump, referring to the crucial Georgia Senate elections, says, "You have a big election coming up, and because of what you've done to the president—you know, the people of Georgia know that this was a scam. Because of what you've done to the president, a lot of people aren't going out to vote, and a lot of Republicans are going to vote negative because they hate what you did to the president."

To finish making his point, Trump tells Raffensperger that he would be "respected, really respected if this can be straightened out before the election." I wonder what he means by "straightened out"! Do I hear you say "corrupt"?

At no point in the call did Trump offer proof of malpractice, let alone fraud. He used expressions like "a lot of people are saying," "there are rumours that," "we have been told." But he never once referred to any concrete evidence—because there is none. Duh! It's all illusory—all smoke and mirrors. Trump is a disgrace.

You may remember Loser Lindsey calling Raffensperger back in mid-November. Raffensperger said he got the impression then that Graham was trying to get him to throw out some of the ballots, a claim Graham denied, but the call was not recorded.

So with lesson learned, when he gets a call from One-Term, he thinks that recording the conversation may not be a bad idea—and that's exactly what happened.

Raffensperger said he would only release the tape if Trump attacked him after the call—and that too is exactly what happened!

Trump tweeted, "I spoke to Secretary of State Brad Raffensperger yesterday. He was unwilling, or unable, to answer questions such as the 'ballots under table' scam, ballot destruction, out-of-state 'voters,' dead voters, and more. He has no clue!" Trump is clearly struggling.

This call is somewhat reminiscent of what led to Trump's first impeachment, the proceedings for which began in mid-January 2020. It started in September 2019, when it came to light that in a July phone call to Ukrainian president Volodymyr Zelensky, Trump had threatened to withhold US aid from Ukraine unless Zelensky agreed to investigate Joe Biden's son, Hunter, for his activities in that country.

At the time, Joe Biden was considered by Trump to be his biggest threat to reelection, so he sought to neutralise the threat by discrediting Biden.

There were plenty of witnesses at the trial who said that Trump did in fact threaten to hold back foreign aid to Ukraine, and it was clear that was exactly what he did. But there was no direct evidence—such as a taped phone call!

Frankly, even if there had been a taped call, I still don't think the Republicans would have found the courage to impeach Trump, with one exception—Mitt Romney. Romney was a presidential candidate in 2008, who lost the Republican nomination to John McCain, who in turn lost the presidential election to Barack Obama.

Romney, a Mormon, is deeply religious and says his faith determines his actions, confirming it was his faith that led him to vote in favour of Trump's impeachment the first time round.

He knew Trump was 100 percent guilty, so he had no choice. Cynics will say Romney has enough money (he's a multimillionaire) to allow him to vote however he wants, but it cannot have been easy for him to be the only Republican to vote in favour of Trump's impeachment.

Wednesday, 6 January 2021—A Truly Sad Day in the History of America

To state the obvious, films will be made about the events of today. It was that momentous. Sadly, it is this that will be Trump's legacy.

In scenes that have to be seen to be believed, we watch pro-Trump demonstrators on the second day of a Save America rally turn into a mob and storm the Capitol. These events take place on the same day that the Electoral College votes are being counted in the Capitol Building in front of a joint session of Congress.

The day begins with demonstrators gathering outside the White House to listen to a bunch of idiot speakers, one of whom is Tweedledumb. He delivers a rambling expletive-laden speech, saying, "You can be a hero, or you can be a zero. And the choice is yours. But we are all watching. The whole world is watching, folks. Choose wisely."

The crowd loves it and chants, "Fight for Trump! Fight for Trump!" He says of the Republicans who had done nothing to "stop the steal," "This gathering should send a message to them. This isn't their Republican Party anymore! This is Donald Trump's Republican Party!" Doesn't that just sum up what a total dick he is?

Other speakers there to stoke up the crowd include Tweedledumber and his wife, plus other family members and Trump sycophants, including the now-disgraced Rudy Giuliani who pathetically calls for "trial by combat." This wanker is well past his "prosecute by date" and needs to be disbarred.

Later in the morning, One-Term himself turns up, adding more fuel to the fire already lit by his family and others. His speech is extraordinary and, as usual, is a string of lies.

He says "And after this, we're going to walk down there [Pennsylvania Avenue], and I'll be there with you. [He wasn't.] We're going to walk down to the Capitol, and we are going to cheer on our brave senators and congressmen and women because you'll never take back our country with weakness. You have to show strength, and you have to be strong."

Before the speeches are over, Trump's family leaves, and Trump heads back into the White House to watch on television the results of what he, Rudy Giuliani, his idiot sons, and others have started.

It's is almost beyond credulity to think that a sitting president of the United States of America can be directly responsible for inciting a mob to commit what Democratic leaders describe as an act of insurrection, but that's exactly what happened.

Trump has been putting Pence under increasing pressure in recent days to not accept the electoral vote count, which is taking place at the same time, and seems to believe that if Pence rejects the numbers, he will gain an election victory through a recount.

But unknown to Trump, Pence has already decided to do the right thing and released a letter to Congress, saying in part, "It is my considered judgment that my oath to support and defend the Constitution constrains me from claiming unilateral authority to determine which electoral votes should be counted and which should not."

When Trump finds out, he tweets, "Mike Pence didn't have the courage to do what should have been done to protect our Country and our Constitution, giving States a chance to certify a corrected set of facts, not the fraudulent or inaccurate ones which they were asked to previously certify." Amazing!

What makes this all the more extraordinary is that Pence has backed Trump every step of the way; he has supported his every crazy idea and has been as loyal as any puppy. And this is the thanks he gets. It just goes to show that you can never do enough for Trump. He will drop you at your first failure to do his bidding.

I can't imagine Pence is surprised, and I can't imagine he liked Trump much in the first place. But as much as I am no fan of Pence, he did not deserve to be treated like this. What Trump did was appalling, but Pence does at least deserve to be congratulated for surviving so long, and for doing the right thing.

While this is going on, the mob fights its way into the Capitol, forcing the Congress joint session to halt the counting of the electoral votes and forcing people throughout the building either to barricade themselves in, wherever they are, or take whatever cover they can. It is a shameful scene to witness.

We see that the House chamber doors have been barricaded from the inside and four plainclothes police officers stand with pistols pointed at rioters through the glass in the doors. Those Congress members who have not left the room take cover behind seats.

I cannot convey how extraordinary and heartbreaking it is to witness such scenes unfold live on television at the nation's capital.

Outside the Capitol Building, we see a clearly insufficient number of police struggling valiantly, but in vain, to keep the mob at bay. Immediately outside one of the entrances, it becomes clear the mob has heard of Trump's tweet about Pence, and we hear shouts of "Hang Mike Pence! Hang Mike Pence!" Then out of nowhere, a makeshift gallows appears. Preplanning? Somebody tell me this isn't really happening.

The crowd has worked itself into a frenzy, and nothing is going to stop them. Some have already infiltrated other parts of the building and are set on mayhem and destruction, which is exactly what they do as they destroy and steal property.

The behaviour of some looks like they are totally out of control as they scream "USA! USA! This is our country." Others are chanting, "Stop the steal." They call themselves patriots, but they're not. This is not the way patriots behave.

Just when you think it can't get worse, it does. One of the rioters, trying to gain access to a room guarded by police, ignores instructions to keep back, and as she tries to force her way in, she is shot and killed. This is America, and this is happening inside the Capitol Building. There are no words to describe these events.

In total, five people die: the rioter in the Capitol; three others, who die of medical emergencies; and the fifth, a police officer, who dies the following day after confronting rioters and whose death is being investigated as possible murder.

The Aftermath

In the days after, two more Capitol police officers who had been at the riot took their own lives.

As we look back on that shameful day, there are countless outstanding questions why the security was so lax, and investigations are beginning to establish where responsibility lies.

Comparisons on security taken are being made to the Black Lives Matter demonstrations in DC earlier this year, when preparations for that event were made such that law enforcement was out in huge numbers and armed to the teeth with guns and tear gas.

A lot needs to be uncovered here; but what is apparent is there was no structured coordination between the law enforcement agencies, the intelligence agencies, and the Department of Defense.

To make matters worse, it transpires that internet postings, starting several months ago, called for action at the rally. Some posts asked people to bring guns, one reading, "This is America. Fuck DC. It's in the Constitution. Bring your goddamn guns." Another said, "We'll storm offices and physically remove and even kill all the DC traitors."

Two days before the riot, one website called for protesters to "stop the steal and execute the 'stealers.'"

Donald J. Trump, president of the United States, needs to be held accountable for his role in this. He is a disgrace to his former office, and I hope in the future he is never allowed to run for public office.

The Georgia Runoff Senate Elections

Oh yes, the runoff elections! What should have been the story of the day was sadly relegated to an afterthought. Trump had been relentless in condemning all the senior Georgia Republicans for their refusal to do anything to overturn the results, and they and their families all received threats from Trump fanatics. So the outcome of the 5 January elections was eagerly awaited.

Waking up on the morning of 6 January, not knowing of the events that would later unfold, I was relieved to have reached the point where we were finally to get a clear view of what lay ahead for Biden's administration.

The previous day had ended well for the Democrats and for the Black community, with Reverend Raphael Warnock securing a landmark victory by becoming the first Black senator ever to be elected in Georgia and only the eleventh to be elected to the Senate.

The final results become known later in the day with Jon Ossoff winning the second Senate seat for the Democrats, thus giving each party fifty seats and therefore the majority to the Democrats, by virtue of Kamala Harris, having the casting vote.

Like Warnock, Ossoff achieves his own first by being the first Jewish senator from Georgia and, at thirty-three years of age, being the youngest member of the Senate since Joe Biden himself was elected in 1973.

What seemed an unlikely victory at one time has finally been achieved and gives Biden a slightly easier path to pushing through his agenda and getting Senate approval for his cabinet and other nominees.

The importance of this victory for the Democratic Party cannot be overstated as the last time any Democrat won a Senate seat in Georgia was with Zell Miller in 2000; and the last time Democrats flipped the state was in 1992, when Bill Clinton won.

Biden Nominates Attorney General

One day after the siege, Joe Biden announces Judge Merrick Garland as his nominee for AG and other prosecutors for the Department of Justice. Garland is well-known and widely respected by Democrats and Republicans alike.

Biden immediately separates his approach from Trump's by saying, "I want to be clear to those who lead this department who you will serve: you won't work for me. You are not the president's or the vice president's lawyer. Your loyalty is not to me."

What adds a note of irony to this appointment is that it was Garland who Barack Obama nominated for the Supreme Court but whose hearing was refused by Mitch McConnell, pending the then upcoming election. Now McConnell can only watch.

Lindsey Graham Gets His

You don't need me to tell you, but yes, Loser Lindsey has flipped again. Following the siege on the Capitol and speaking at the joint session of Congress to count the Electoral College votes, he said, "Trump and I, we've had a hell of a journey. He's been a consequential president. All I can say is count me out. Enough is enough."

In saying that, he became one of the first rats to leave that sinking rudderless ship that is One-Term Trump.

He even acknowledged Biden's victory, saying that "Joe Biden and Kamala Harris are lawfully elected and will become the president and the vice president of the United States on January 20."

But sadly for Flip-Flop, he was shouted at two days later at Reagan National Airport when leaving to go back to North Carolina. A group of about a dozen people gathered around him shouting "traitor" because he had not tried to block the Electoral College votes.

One woman, who had been more active than most, told him among the shouts, "It's going to be like this forever wherever you go for the rest of your life!"

The following day, Graham decided it would be better to be back in the Trump camp and, referring to his experience at the airport, said, "I know people are frustrated. I wanted President Trump to win so badly. I think he made the world safer and more prosperous." So the flip-flop lasted all of two days, but don't worry, Lindsey. We knew it was only a matter of time before you did it again.

Trump Says He Will Not Attend Biden's Inauguration

Boo-hoo! Poor Porky Don. He is so cross he lost the game that he says he doesn't want to play anymore and will not go to nasty Joey's party on 20 January—so there!

Frankly, that's one of the best decisions this pathetulant has made in four years, but in truth, it confirms what type of person he is and how he lacks any a semblance of moral fibre.

Trust me, Don, not only will America be better off without you, but the whole world will sleep better knowing your presidential decisions will no longer be a matter of consequence. And America can rejoice in the knowledge you will no longer be able to further balls up its international reputation.

You are politically and intellectually inept and devoid of even the remotest understanding of what is good for your country. But I suppose at least your mother loved you. But did she? She apparently once said of you, "Yes, he's an idiot with zero common sense and no social skills, but he *is* my son. I just hope he never goes into politics. He'd be a disaster."

Well, she was right. You are not, nor were you ever, the answer to this county's difficulties. The only question to which you are the answer is "Who is the worst president in America's history?"

Post-Riot Fallout for Tweetless Trump

It should come as no surprise that Trump is being held responsible for what happened, because he is—100 percent. He has not had much to say since; but on the day of the rally-turned-riot, he waited a full two hours after the rioting started to release a video message, asking his followers to stop and return home.

He said, "I know your pain. I know you're hurt. But you have to go home now." He continued his attack on the election and told his supporters, "We can't play into the hands of these people. We love you. You're very special." Pass me the tissues!

And to prove how totally detached he is from reality, he tweeted that evening, "These are the things and events that happen when a sacred landslide election victory is so unceremoniously & viciously stripped away from great patriots who have been badly & unfairly treated for so long."

What sacred landslide victory? Biden won, you moron—and by a landslide, at least by your standards of measurement. And presumably, "the great patriots" are those who rioted and chanted, "Hang Mike Pence."

All of this has consequences for Trump with nine resignations so far, including two cabinet members—Betsy de Vos, secretary of education, and Elaine Chao, transport secretary. Chao is Mitch McConnell's wife.

Another among those leaving is Mick Mulvaney, special envoy to Northern Ireland and former acting chief of staff. Initially, there was speculation that more resignations would follow, but according to Mulvaney, many would like to leave but "are choosing to stay because they're worried the president might put someone worse in."

To add to Trump's woes, he has been suspended from Twitter, Facebook, Instagram, and about a dozen other social media platforms. Twitter's suspension is permanent, but some others are temporary for the moment.

Not being confronted with his asinine tweets every day is another reason for me to wake up smiling. Whilst the suspensions are welcome, many politicians are saying they are long overdue and accuse the larger names—such as Twitter, Facebook, etc.—of putting income before morals and of having enabled Trump. They may well be right, but the damage is already done.

As if that's not enough for One-Term, the Democrats want Mike Pence to implement the Twenty-Fifth Amendment, which says that if the president becomes unable to do his job, then the vice president becomes the president or acting president. Frankly, Trump has never been able to do his job, but the Dems are saying if Pence does not go for the Twenty-Fifth Amendment, they will impeach him for a second time.

It gets better all the time.

Why Republicans Must Impeach Trump

The last time Democrats moved to impeach Trump, no House Republican supported the motion. But Democrats had the House majority, so the motion was passed anyway. But when the impeachment vote went to the Senate, only Mitt Romney voted with the Democrats.

This time, it's different because Democrats and Republicans alike agree that the events of 6 January 2021 were shameful. Almost all believe the president is responsible, and more Republican senators support impeachment this time. But will the numbers be enough to achieve the necessary two-thirds majority? Republicans currently have a fifty-two to forty-eight majority in the Senate.

Frankly, I cannot understand why any Republican would be reluctant to impeach. They should be the ones instigating it. If Trump is found guilty, then he won't be able to stand for office again, although that will require a separate Senate vote. So it has to be in their best interest to be shot of him, especially now.

The sooner his involvement with the party becomes part of its history, the better. But perhaps not everyone sees it that way. Perhaps they're worried about not being reelected or of what the base may do, especially the rabid right element.

If reelection is a concern, Republicans urgently need to reconsider their position because prostituting themselves to protect their seats will come at a huge and lasting cost to their personal and political integrity. Their opinions will have no value and they will find themselves politically stranded.

Far better to stand strong and help rebuild a party with its traditional Republican values. They can then fight for their seats as people of honour instead of self-serving wimps with no concern for what is good for their country.

Wishful thinking? Of course it is, but at the moment the Republican party is on a fast track to self-destruction and that's not good for anyone.

As it is, after the House votes to impeach, seventeen Republican senators will need to find Trump guilty—assuming the Senate sits after inauguration day—to achieve the magic number of sixty-seven.

But just imagine what a prize Republicans would give themselves if they voted "en masse" to find him guilty. They would have safety in numbers (a different kind of herd immunity, perhaps). And their message would be crystal clear: "Trump lied. The election was fair. He incited violence!"

And it might even be a wake-up call for some of Trump's true base. I believe, perhaps perversely, that the bigger the majority guilty verdict, the better it will be for the Republican Party's future.

The worst of all worlds is that Trump is impeached by the House but again is acquitted by the Senate. Should that happen, he would be empowered and become even more dangerous and destructive than he is already. The House needs to impeach him, and the Senate needs to find him guilty!

Money Talks

Whilst I wasn't expecting it, I suppose I shouldn't be surprised to learn today, 12 January, that a large number of corporates have said as a result of recent events, they will stop making political donations to all lawmakers who opposed Biden's election certification—at least for the time being. Among those companies are American Express, AT&T, Dow Inc., Amazon, and General Electric.

Corporate donations are an important part of each party's funding but are viewed by many as one of the reasons politicians are considered amoral, if not immoral. "If I contribute 'x,' you need to give me 'y'!"

It strikes me that the world would be a better place if corporate donations were forbidden altogether. There is something distinctly sleazy about politicians being for sale. And while we're at it, why not also exclude all large individual donations? Pipe dreams? Certainly, but the world of large political donations is far too opaque and needs a thorough review.

Don't forget that while campaigning in 2015, Trump said he was so rich that he had enough money to fund his own campaign so was not beholden to anyone. Of course, it was again more rubbish because he took money from whoever wanted to contribute, but the message that he was independent of outside influence went down well and earned him a good many supporters.

But will the current suspension of corporate financial support have any effect on the behaviour of the parties and their politicians? Yes, but I'm not sure we'll see it directly. They will certainly be flustered and work behind the scenes to woo back their contributors.

We have already seen some Republicans coming out against Trump, and some had already expressed concerns. Nonetheless, the threat of withdrawal of important funding will always concentrate the mind. Money talks!

The House Impeaches Trump—Again!

Well, it's happened again! Today, 13 January, President Donald J. Trump is impeached a second time. This time for "incitement of insurrection."

In a four-page impeachment bill, it was stated that "President Trump gravely endangered the security of the United States and its institutions of government" and that "he will remain a threat to national security, democracy, and the Constitution if allowed to remain in office." Seems pretty clear!

Trump loves records, and being impeached again makes him the only president to be impeached twice. Nobody deserves such an accolade more than him. What makes today even more special is that ten House Republicans sided with the Democrats to impeach, including Elizabeth Cheney, the third most senior Republican in the House of Representatives.

Also in support was Adam Kinzinger, a forty-two-year-old air force veteran who served as a pilot in Iraq and Afghanistan, among other places. Kinzinger was not happy with some of the military decisions Trump made, especially removing US troops from Northern Syria in October 2019. Even so, his criticism of Trump has been firm but measured.

Kinzinger is impressive, and if he wants it, I'm sure there is a big future ahead for him. He is exactly the type of person the Republican Party needs to restore a sense of normality and Republican values.

He is well-informed, has leadership qualities, and who knows, maybe he and Cheney will be a team one day! But let's not forget the other Republicans who voted for impeachment.[20] They too need to be praised, and they are all later censured by the party. It's hard to believe.

---

[20] Their names need to be recognised as individuals who put themselves second. They are John Katko, New York; Fred Upton, Michigan; Jaime Herrera Beutler, Washington state; Dan Newhouse, Washington state; Anthony Gonzalez, Ohio; Peter Meijer, Michigan; Tom Rice, South Carolina; and David Valadao, California.

Mitch McConnell has said the Senate will not sit before the inauguration date of 20 January, meaning Democrats will need seventeen Senate Republicans to side with them for a guilty verdict.

Getting seventeen Republicans on their side is an extremely a tall order. Some senators have reportedly confided in journalists that if they vote for impeachment, they will lose their seat. We have already seen senators hiding behind the argument that the country needs to heal. Fine, but what about accountability?

If Trump had properly accepted the outcome of the election, it is hard to imagine any of this happening. His supporters would have been upset, but with his cajoling, they would have accepted it.

Dream on! He was never going to go quietly. Even before the 2016 election, he said that if he lost, it would be because of electoral fraud; and even after he won, he still cried fraud because he did not like losing the popular vote to Hillary. Trump has been building up to this and stirring up his supporters for more than four years.

And look where we are today. The Capitol was stormed by rioters. Five people died, and there was large-scale destruction of property. Trump did this, aided and abetted by his lunatic group of election-deniers.

Another major contributory factor is that Trump went unchallenged by fellow Republicans throughout his term, thereby giving him ever-increasing power and complete authority.

His grip over the party has been so strong that even today, senators are scared to go against him. But he must not be given a pass under the guise of the country needing to heal. He must be held accountable.

However, the question is, when should the Senate convene? Speaker Nancy Pelosi declined to say when she would send the article (of impeachment) to the Senate—the step that triggers a trial. But there is so much hate in the air that to hold the trial anytime soon may not end well, no matter what the result.

If Trump is found guilty, there could well be problems for Republican senators finding against him because some House Republicans who voted to impeach have since received threats;

and if he's acquitted, Trump would be supercharged to sow even further division. Welcome to the new America!

Fortress Washington

Following the serious failures of 6 January, security is now on steroids, ahead of the inauguration. The city is in virtual lockdown as eight-foot fencing has been erected in all strategic places, topped with razor wire. Roadblocks are everywhere, making life extremely difficult for local residents.

National Guard troops are streaming into DC, and it is estimated they will total twenty-five thousand before inauguration day—that's more than all the US troops in Afghanistan, Syria, and Iraq combined.

And just in case we thought the capital city would be too well-protected for anyone to risk further acts of violence, police confirmed that a man was arrested yesterday, Friday, 15 January, as he tried to pass through a Capitol Police checkpoint.

He was found to be carrying what was described as an "unauthorized inauguration credential," as well as a loaded handgun and more than five hundred rounds of ammunition.

But remember, all this is happening in the capital of the United States: thousands of troops, high fences topped with razor wire, military vehicles everywhere—and for what? To protect the country against right-wing extremists' intent upon overturning democracy in their own country.

They are domestic terrorists supported and encouraged by none other than the sitting president of the United States; it's as simple and as tragic as that.

And just in case we think it's only DC that faces problems, the FBI has warned of possible armed marches by pro-Trump demonstrators at all fifty state capitol buildings. All I can say is thank goodness we have a Biden presidency to look forward to. Cometh the hour, cometh the man, I hope!

Biden Announces a Raft of Executive Orders

Biden clearly wants to get off to a quick start. He has already announced his plan to achieve one hundred million vaccines in his first hundred days. Trump's aim to get twenty million vaccines into arms by the end of 2020 was an abject failure, but he had long abrogated his presidential responsibilities in favour of the golf course.

Biden has also announced his COVID stimulus plan, which among a wide range of measures to be introduced over a period of about ten days, includes increasing the already Congress-approved $600 payment to $2,000 and expanding it to a broader base. He further plans to announce legislation to allow eleven million illegal immigrants a path to citizenship, but details have yet to be made announced.

Among the executive orders he will sign, one will end the travel ban on predominantly Muslim countries, and another will be a move to rejoin the Paris climate accord. And in line with his fight against coronavirus, he will also impose a mask mandate requiring masks to be worn in all federal buildings and on inter-state travel.

The one thread that runs through all this shows Biden to be the antithesis of Trump, and that's something else for the world to look forward to.

McConnell Holds Trump Responsible

Just two days before Joe Biden's inauguration, Mitch McConnell, Senate majority leader, speaking about the 6 January riots, says that "the mob was fed lies," that they "were provoked by the president and other powerful people, and they tried to use fear and violence to stop a specific proceeding of the first branch of the federal government, which they did not like."

Chuck Schumer, McConnell's successor, says of Trump's behaviour that the Senate needs to set a precedent that the "sever-est offense ever committed by a president would be met by the severest remedy provided by the Constitution—impeachment." He also calls for Trump to be barred from holding future office.

McConnell's comments came as quite a surprise, but they do support reports that he has privately expressed his dislike of Trump. It is also seen as giving free reign to Republican senators to find Trump guilty, but whether they do that is another matter. It's not even clear, despite his words, whether McConnell will vote to convict.

Such is the purity of politics, but I still don't trust McConnell.

Trump's Final Pardons

Just before he left, Trump granted seventy-four pardons and seventy commutations, about forty of which related to nonviolent drug-related crimes, which was good to see, and more than thirty related to financial crimes, which was not so good. A handful of politicians and a couple of rappers benefited, but nothing particularly scandalous.

There was much speculation that Trump may try to pardon himself and family members, but it's reported that his lawyers persuaded him against it as they thought it may prove illegal. Whether legal or not, it would certainly have been controversial. In the end, what was expected to be a much-talked-about final pardon list turned out to be pretty tame.

Trump did however pardon Steve Bannon, his former campaign manager, who was indicted in August 2020 on wire fraud and money laundering conspiracy charges. It was alleged that Bannon, whose "We Build the Wall" campaign that raised some $25 million, had used hundreds of thousands of dollars for personal expenses. I wonder who taught him that trick!

Biden and Harris Are Sworn In

Today, 20 January 2021, is the day when a huge majority of Americans, Mexicans, Canadians, world citizens, and probably

Martians breathe a massive collective sigh of relief as One-Time becomes a former president.

Just a reminder, he lost to Biden by the same "landslide" margin by which he beat Hillary, 306 to 232 seats; but again, he lost the popular vote—this time by an even bigger margin of nearly eight million.

The inauguration ceremony was unlike any seen in modern times, with COVID influencing every aspect. Even so, the event still had its highlights, one of the most notable being the reciting of a poem by the country's first National Youth Poet Laureate, twenty-two-year-old Amanda Gorman. Extremely impressive.

Biden's speech was a breath of fresh air. He wasn't full of bombast. He wasn't brash, and best of all, he wasn't Trump. Tackling coronavirus is his priority. Getting that under control will provide the fuel necessary to get the economy moving forward again, he argued.

He talked about repairing alliances and engaging with the world again, promising, "We will lead not merely by the example of our power—by the power of our example."

Overall, Biden's speech was much of what we might have expected; but the air was made all the fresher by the absence of One-Term, who, after four years of lies and BS, had left Andrews Air Force Base earlier in the morning to strains of Frank Sinatra's "I Did It My Way."

It was pathetic. It would have been much better if they had played Tom Petty's "Don't Come Around Here No More."

Finally! He's Out

I remain bewildered that anyone could have voted for Trump in 2016 but dumbfounded that even more people voted for him in 2020. He is, by a mile, the worst modern-day president this country has had and probably, the worst ever.

It therefore gives me great pleasure to announce the full-time score:

Impeachments—2
Terms in office—1
Here endeth the Trump presidency!

COVID-19: One Year On

Biden's inauguration marks the first anniversary of the first case of coronavirus being recorded in the US, and in that single year, we have twenty-five million reported cases and 412,000 deaths. Cases have recently been recorded at the rate of one million in five days with a staggering three hundred thousand cases in a single day on 8 January. Hospitalisations remain above one hundred thousand, and we have seen a number of days when deaths have exceeded 4,000.

Words like *tragic, shocking, heartbreaking* don't even begin to capture the horror of this; and yet there are still people who refuse to wear a mask, claiming it's an infringement of their personal rights. I really don't understand.

But amid this misery, there may be some good news. One of the contributing causes to the increase in numbers was due to people travelling over Thanksgiving, Christmas, and New Year. However, these holidays are now behind us, and rate of new cases is reducing.

Hospitalisations and deaths will always lag, but there is hope-again-that we may have reached the peak. However, we still face further risks from the more contagious variant from the UK, plus a South African variant, and now one from Brazil.

Biden's First Days in Office

Whilst the new administration's major emphasis remains tackling coronavirus, President Biden's opening days in office are defined by his signing twenty-eight executive orders in eight days, many of which have reversed decisions made by Trump, one notably lifting Trump's ban on transgender individuals serving in the military and another reintroducing travel restrictions lifted by Trump before leaving office.

Beginning Monday, 25 January, Biden's executive orders had a daily theme, starting with "Buy America," followed by racial equity, then the climate crisis, health care, and, on Friday, immigration. In doing this, he is showing where his priorities are while clearly separating himself from everything Trumpian.

Biden has received some criticism for targeting one hundred million vaccines in his first one hundred days in office. This is considered an easily achievable target and needs to be at least twice or even three times that pace to ensure adequate levels of immunisation.

Article of Impeachment Delivered to Senate

On Monday, 25 January, at around 7:00 p.m., history was again made as the article of impeachment was delivered to the Senate, but there was something of a Greek tragedy about the whole proceeding as we watched the prosecution team make their way through the Capitol Building through areas where violence took place.

Political reporters from all media are saying they have been told privately by a number of Republican senators that they hold Trump responsible for the riots but will not vote that way, so the likelihood of Trump being found guilty as charged looks remote right now. The trial will begin in two weeks, so we will see then how things pan out.

An amusing sidenote is that Trump is having some difficulty pulling together a legal team to defend him. Some firms reportedly simply do not want be associated with him—which is hard to believe as I would have thought there would be countless "ambulance-chasers" to step up.

Others have reportedly passed on the opportunity as they are concerned they would not get paid. Now, that's a lot more believable, given Trump's track record. He's even said he will not pay

Giuliani because he failed in his attempts to overturn the election results!

And talking of Raving Rudy, he's being sued for $1.3 billion dollars for defamation by Dominion Voting Systems, the people who produced the vote-counting machines. *The New York Times* reports Dominion has filed a 107-page lawsuit, accusing Giuliani of carrying out "a viral disinformation campaign about Dominion" made up of "demonstrably false" allegations in part to enrich himself through legal fees and his podcast. Love it!

Is COVID-19 on the Turn?

January closes with the highest recorded number of US deaths in a single month at nearly 100,000; but despite this bad news, we learn that daily case numbers are declining, which hopefully is an encouraging sign. However, it's worth recognising that total cases are above 26.5 million and total deaths exceed 450,000.

February 2021

Huge Snowstorm Hits New York

February started in style! On 2 February, more than seventeen inches of snow fell in New York City. It looked beautiful and majestic, but sadly not for long. As the snowploughs pushed piles of snow to the sides of the road, any romantic notions of being in a winter-wonderland were soon dispelled. However, Central Park held on to its beauty for longer than most places.

We All Have One…

All families have at least one member they don't like to talk about, and it's the same with political parties. Both the Democratic and Republican Parties have a handful of members they wish would quietly go away.

The Democrats have a small group of self-described democratic socialists, one of whom, Alexandria Ocasio-Cortez, is probably top of their shortlist. AOC, as she is known, is a New Yorker, who is a little too far left for comfort, but, who at thirty-one years old, is not only young but eloquent, persuasive, well-informed and very smart. So it's not easy to dismiss her as irrelevant or crazy—she's neither.

AOC and her cohort are definitely a thorn in the side of the Democratic mainstream, and with majorities in both houses being so narrow, their voices have become louder. I'm just not sure their politics are what the Democratic Party needs right now.

AOC and friends do have a following, and they can make life very uncomfortable for their party, especially at election time. But they also need to be listened to.

As for the Republicans, their top-of-list really is crazy. She is one Marjorie Taylor Greene, who became a congresswoman only in January this year. There is much that can be said about her, but in short, she's a conspiracy theorist and a racist.

Among the conspiracy theories she supports is one that Bill and Hillary Clinton have killed fifty or more of their associates. She has supported those charming far-right activists QAnon, who allege that a secret cabal of Satan-worshipping cannibalistic paedophiles is running a global child sex-trafficking ring.

She says that the fatal shootings at Sandy Hook and Parkland schools in 2012 and 2018, respectively, were staged events, that the 2017 Las Vegas shooting and killing of fifty-nine people and the injuring of more than five hundred was inspired by Democrats looking to introduce gun-control measures, and—let's not forget—that the California fires of 2018 were started by laser beams fired from outer space and funded by Jews. Of course they were, dear. But guess what? Trump thinks she's great!

There were many calls for her to be stripped of her seats on the Education and Budget Committees, which Republicans eventually put to a vote. The vote went in her favour, and she was even given a standing ovation by some after her speech!

The Democrats, however, were not satisfied and, on 3 February, held a vote among all House members. Result? She lost. The vote count against her was 230 (including 11 Republicans) to 199, and she lost her committee assignments. This was a pathetic show by Republicans, so scared of Trump that the majority of them left their morals at home, leaving it up to the Democrats to do their dirty work for them.

A good share of blame for this mess lies at the feet of Kevin McCarthy, minority leader of the House. He had obviously been taking lessons from Loser "Flip-Flop" Graham. First, McCarthy said Trump was responsible for the events of 6 January, then he said he wasn't. Then everyone was responsible, then he said he never said Trump was responsible. Then he went to Mar-a-Lago to kiss Trump's arse, then all was well with Marjorie Greene. Get the picture?

Here, I should also briefly mention Matt Gaetz (pronounced Gates) who, like Greene, is new to congress and, like Greene, is a nutter. He's also a super-sleaze, and I write more on him a little later.

Super Bowl: A Super-Spreader?

I thought we had seen the last of large gatherings, but seeing so many people in Tampa Bay gather closely together without masks to celebrate Sunday's victory of the Tampa Bay Buccaneers over the Kansas City Chiefs by thirty-one to nine proves that some people either don't care or they're reckless or they're just plain stupid.

The stadium has a capacity of 66,000, but only 25,000 fans—7,500 of whom were vaccinated health workers—were allowed to attend. There has been so much done to get on top of COVID that to see people get together in such numbers is infuriating. The only consolation is that they were outside, so that will limit any spread of the virus.

Liz Cheney Fights Back

Since voting in January with Democrats to impeach Trump, Cheney, the third most senior Republican in the House, has been given a hard time by Trump loyalists. So much so that they called for her expulsion from party leadership and, on 3 February, forced a secret ballot on whether she should retain her number-three position.

She won that vote comfortably by 145 to 61, but 61 in favour of her expulsion is not insignificant. I wonder if that number would have been higher had the vote been public.

Not satisfied with Cheney surviving the expulsion vote, her own Wyoming state's Republican Party asked her to resign her seat and decided on Saturday she should be censured, approving a censure resolution by fifty-six to eight votes. The resolution stated the state party would not raise money for her in the future, and she was asked to repay state party's 2020 campaign donations made to her.

Undaunted by Republicans' criticism of her, the next day, she appeared on Fox News Sunday hosted by Chris Wallace, telling him that the GOP will have lost its way if it doesn't reject Trump's brand of politics. She said, "The extent to which President Trump, for months leading up to 6 January, spread the notion that the election had been stolen or that the election was rigged was a lie. And people need to understand that."

Cheney did not hesitate to defend her decision to impeach Trump and, to respond to criticism from within her own party, sought to address her constituents, saying, "I think people all across Wyoming understand and recognise that our most important duty is to the Constitution." She went on to say, "The oath that I took to the Constitution compelled me to vote for impeachment, and it doesn't bend to partisanship. It doesn't bend to political pressure."

She also didn't hesitate to criticise Trump, saying, "He was not only a bad leader for the Republicans to embrace but also posed an existential threat to the nation." She added, "The single greatest threat to our republic is a president who would put his own self-interest above the Constitution, above the national interest, and we've had a situation where President Trump claimed for months that the election was stolen and then apparently set about to do everything he could to steal it himself."

In today's political world, we could do with a few more Liz Cheneys. Doing what she has done amid such extreme partisanship is both brave and impressive.

But Chris Cillizza, writing for CNN, says, "Democrats praising Cheney for her principled stands on Trump would do well to remember that she is no Democrat. She is anti-Trump but not at all pro-Biden."

Trump's Second Impeachment Trial

Big surprise—not guilty! Of course, the vote was to acquit—but it was nonetheless historic. The result was a fifty-seven to forty-three numerical victory for the Democrats with an unprecedented seven Republicans finding Trump guilty, but Democrats still fell ten votes shy of the sixty-seven votes needed for a conviction.

However, we need to be realistic. By the time it started, the trial was a foregone conclusion, especially with people like Cretin Cruz and Loser Lindsey going in with the attitude "I'll listen carefully to all the evidence, then I'll acquit."

Suffice to say, the prosecution team was detailed, methodical, and convincing, whereas the defence were not up to the task. Trump's lawyers had no relevant experience and were defending a client who, by any standard, was guilty but would be acquitted anyway. Meanwhile, the prosecution had an abundance of evidence supporting their case, all of which would be ignored by most Republican senators.

However, before commenting on the trial, I think it is relevant to highlight chronologically some of the events of 6 January and part of 7 January to show how the situation unfolded and to see what Trump did and, more particularly, didn't do.

Wednesday, 6 January

8:17 a.m., Trump tweets allegations of vote fraud, stating, "States want to correct their votes, which they now know were based on irregularities and fraud, plus corrupt process never received legislative approval. All Mike Pence has to do is send them back to the States, AND WE WIN. Do it Mike, this is a time for extreme courage!"

12:00 p.m., Trump begins his over-one-hour speech, repeating allegations that the election was stolen, criticising Mike Pence by name a half dozen times, accusing fellow Republicans of not doing enough to back up his allegations.

12:30 p.m., crowds of pro-Trump supporters, including members of the right wing-extremist group, Proud Boys, gather outside the US Capitol Building.

12:53 p.m., rioters overwhelm police along the outer perimeter west of the Capitol Building.

1:05 p.m., Congress meets in a joint session to confirm Joe Biden's electoral victory.

1:09 p.m., Capitol Police Chief Sund asks House and Senate sergeants at arms to declare an emergency and call for deployment of the National Guard. They agree to forward the request up their respective chains of command.

1:10 p.m., Trump ends his speech by encouraging the crowd to march to the Capitol: "We're going to try and give them [Republicans] the kind of pride and boldness that they need to take back our country." He returns to the White House immediately after the speech.

1:30 p.m., Capitol Police are forced to retreat up the steps of the Capitol. Large numbers of Trump supporters march from the Ellipse—the place where Trump gave his speech 1.5 miles away.

1:34 p.m., DC mayor Muriel Bowser formally requests more federal assistance to deal with the mob.

1:49 p.m., Chief Sund requests immediate assistance from the National Guard.

1:59 p.m., Sund receives the first reports that rioters had reached the Capitol's doors and windows and were trying to break in.

2:05 p.m., Kevin Greeson is declared dead after suffering a heart attack on the Capitol grounds. Gleeson was a former Democrat, who became a radical Trump fanatic. On 17 December, he had written on social media, "Let's take this fucking Country BACK!! Load your guns and take to the streets!"

2:10 p.m., the mob west of the Capitol chases police up the steps, breaching the final barricade, and approaches an entrance directly below the Senate chamber. House sergeant at arms Irving calls Chief Sund with formal approval to request assistance from the National Guard. This call for assistance comes a staggering one hour after the initial request. Both Irving and Senate Sergeant at Arms Michael Stenger were to resign the following day.

Also at 2:10 p.m., text and email alerts are sent to all congressional staff, warning those inside to stay away from windows and those outside to seek cover.

2:12 p.m., the first rioter enters the Capitol through the broken window, opening a door for others.

2:13 p.m., Mike Pence is removed from the Senate chamber, and the Senate is called into recess.

2:14 p.m., rioters chase a lone Capitol Police officer, Eugene Goodman, up flights of stairs, where there are doors to the Senate chamber in both directions. Goodman leads the mob away from Senate doors while senators inside attempt to evacuate.

2:15 p.m., insurgents shout, "Hang Mike Pence!"

2:18 p.m., another text alert goes out to Capitol staff: "Due to security threat inside, immediately move inside your office, take emergency equipment, lock the doors, take shelter."

2:24 p.m., Trump tweets, "Mike Pence didn't have the courage to do what should have been done to protect our Country and our Constitution, giving States a chance to certify a corrected set of facts, not the fraudulent or inaccurate ones which they were asked to previously certify. USA demands the truth!" His tweet is read out over a megaphone to the rioters.

2:26 p.m., Pence and family evacuated to new secure location.

Also at 2:26 p.m., Police Chief Sund joins a conference call with several officials from the DC government, as well as officials from the Pentagon, including Lieutenant General Walter Piatt, director of the army staff. Sund says, "I am making an urgent, urgent immediate request for National Guard assistance. I have got to get boots on the ground." The DC contingent is flabbergasted when Piatt refuses to pass on the request to his superior, Army Secretary McCarthy, saying, "I don't like the visual of the National Guard standing a police line with the Capitol in the background."

2:28 p.m., Sund repeats his request for National Guard support to help shore up the perimeter of the Capitol.

2:33 p.m., a broadcast on the emergency management agency channel in DC requests that all law enforcement officers in the city respond to the Capitol.

2:38 p.m., President Trump tweets, "Please support our Capitol Police and Law Enforcement. They are truly on the side of our Country. Stay peaceful!" Trump apparently needed a lot of persuading to add "stay peaceful" to his tweet, according to his aides.

2:44 p.m., pro-Trump rioter Ashli Babbitt is fatally shot by Capitol Police while attempting to force entry into the Speaker's Lobby adjacent to the House chambers.

2:52 p.m., the first FBI SWAT team enters the Capitol.

3:04 p.m., formal approval for full activation of the 1,100 soldiers in the DC National Guard. Most of activated guardsmen would require two hours to leave their jobs and homes and equip themselves at the DC Armory.

Note: At this point, it is more than ninety minutes since Mayor Bowser first asked Army secretary McCarthy for assistance. It took an hour for Defense Department officials to meet and another half hour for them to decide to help, and yet Bowser still doesn't know the status of her request.

3:13 p.m., Trump tweets, "I am asking for everyone at the US Capitol to remain peaceful. No violence! Remember, WE are the Party of Law & Order—respect the Law and our great men and women in Blue. Thank you!"

3:26 p.m., Army secretary McCarthy calls Bowser to tell her that her request for help has been approved. The Defense

Department's notification of approval to Bowser came two hours after her request.

3:37 p.m., Maryland National Guard is mobilised in anticipation of a request for support.

3:46 p.m., chief of the National Guard Bureau is informed that Virginia National Guard forces have already been mobilized.

4:17 p.m., Trump uploads a video to his Twitter, saying, "I know your pain. I know you're hurt. We had an election that was stolen from us. It was a landslide election, and everyone knows it, especially the other side. But you have to go home now. We have to have peace. We have to have law and order. We have to respect our great people in law and order. We don't want anybody hurt. It's a very tough period of time. There's never been a time like this where such a thing happened where they could take it away from all of us—from me, from you, from our country. This was a fraudulent election, but we can't play into the hands of these people. We have to have peace. So go home. We love you. You're very special. You've seen what happens. You see the way others are treated that are so bad and so evil. I know how you feel, but go home. And go home in peace." Seriously? You can't make this stuff up!

4:26 p.m., Rosanne Boyland is trampled to death by rioters at a Capitol tunnel entrance while police are attacked. She is pronounced dead at a local hospital at 6:09 p.m.

5:40 p.m., 154 National Guard soldiers arrive at the Capitol Complex, swear in with the Capitol Police, and begin support operations.

Around 5:40 p.m., as the interior of the Capitol is cleared of rioters, leaders of Congress state that they will continue tallying electoral votes.

Around 5:45 p.m., police announce that Ashli Babbitt, the rioter shot inside the Capitol, has died.

6:01 p.m., Trump tweets, "These are the things and events that happen when a sacred landslide election victory is so unceremoniously & viciously stripped away from great patriots who have been badly & unfairly treated for so long. Go home with love & in peace. Remember this day forever!" Total wanker!

8:00 p.m., US Capitol Police declare the Capitol Building to be secure.

8:06 p.m., the Senate reconvenes with Pence presiding to continue debating the objection to the Arizona electoral count (more than one hundred Republicans had moved to reject the results of electoral votes in two states, first Arizona, then Pennsylvania).

Thursday, 7 January

The House and the Senate debate and vote separately, and it's not until three ten in the morning of 7 January that the objections to the electoral votes of both Arizona and Pennsylvania are rejected by the House and the Senate.

At 3:24 a.m., Congress completes the counting of the electoral votes with Biden winning—306–232. Accordingly, VP Pence affirms the election result, formally declaring Joe Biden the winner.

Around 9:30 p.m., Capitol Police officer Brian Sicknick dies after being injured by rioters the previous day.

The Trial Begins: 9 February 2021

The prosecution team led by Jamie Raskin, whose twenty-five-year-old son had tragically taken his own life one week before the riot, expertly showed how Trump started building up to 6 January long before that date, citing his repeated whining that if he were to lose the election, it would be due to fraud.

Indeed, as I mentioned earlier, this was Trump's cry even before the election he won, so he definitely had history. And Raskin and his team tease out the facts.

The prosecution led us step-by-step through the events leading up to that fateful day. We saw previously unseen videos of what took place, highlighting the rioters' extreme level of violence and giving us a sense of the terror those under siege were feeling, many of whom had barricaded themselves into offices.

We learnt from David Cicilline, one of the House impeachment managers, that at least 138 law enforcement officers were injured—73 Capitol Police officers and 65 officers from the Metropolitan Police Department.

The chairman of the Capitol Police Labour Committee said, in part, "I have officers who were not issued helmets prior to the attack who have sustained brain injuries. One officer has two cracked ribs and two smashed spinal discs. One officer is going to lose his eye, and another was stabbed with a metal fence stick."

Cicilline spoke of officers suffering "concussions, irritated lungs, injuries caused by repeated blows from bats, poles, and clubs," adding that these officers "sustained injuries that will be with them for the rest of their lives."

So much of this could have been avoided had Trump called off the rioters much earlier.

There is a lot more colour that can be added, but significant are the tweets sent by Trump and the timing of them. He knew what was happening but did nothing to stop it

Indeed he refused to stop it; and we learnt from the prosecution that a Republican senator (Ben Sasse, but not named at the trial) had been told by senior White House officials that Trump was "delighted" to hear that his supporters were breaking into the Capitol Building and that he "was walking around the White House, confused about why other people on his team weren't as excited as he was."

Without detailing all the communications between the Defence Department, National Guard, the army secretary, et al., it is clear a number of individuals with authority to deploy or recommend deployment of forces to defend the Capitol did not react well to the pressure they were under; and clearly many decisions could have been taken sooner.

Just as extraordinary, on the fifth and final day of the trial, when we were expecting to hear closing arguments, lead prosecutor Jamie Raskin said he would like to call a witness, Jaime Herrera

Beutler, a Republican House member, who was one of the ten to vote in favour of Trump's impeachment.

She was prepared to give evidence detailing what House minority leader Kevin McCarthy said took place in a heated conversation he had with Trump during the riot.

The defence team were taken completely off guard and protested vigorously. Proceedings were halted while discussions took place on how best to play this. Neither side wanted a protracted trial, and this could well add days, if not weeks.

It was agreed that rather than calling on Herrera Beutler to give evidence, her statement would be read into the record, part of which reads,

> When McCarthy finally reached the president on January 6th and asked him to publicly and forcefully call off the riot, the president initially repeated the falsehood that it was Antifa that had breached the Capitol. McCarthy refuted that and told the president that these were Trump supporters. That's when, according to McCarthy, the president said well Kevin, I guess these people are more upset about the election than you are.

What was not included in the statement was McCarthy's reply to Trump's rebuke. He told Herrera Beutler and others that he said to Trump, "Who the fuck do you think you're talking to?" Maybe that's why he had to go to Mar-a-Lago to kiss arse!

The Closing Arguments

The closing arguments came and went. The prosecution team used ten of the sixteen hours available and hit all the right notes, their pleadings were moving and compelling. They showed how the events of 6 January were a culmination of what had begun months before, and that the timing of Trump's speech was no accident. It was not only planned but planned for that day.

One particular remark that resonated was made by Joe Neguse, the son of Eritrean immigrants and, at thirty-six, the youngest member of the team. He referred to defence counsel's "continued references to hate" and cited Martin Luther King Jr., who said, "I have decided to stick with love. Hate is too great a burden to bear." Then addressing the defence team directly, he added, "This trial is not born from hate, far from it. It is born of love of country."

The defence team was far less convincing, but they had precious little to work with. They characterised Trump as a "law and order" president, saying the charges were brought "as an act of vengeance" and that it was "a politically motived witch hunt."

Their performances were weak, ensuring they will not be on our screens again anytime soon. The only thing that came across with any force was that they tried to echo Trump whenever they could; and there they succeeded as just like Trump, they lied their way to the very end. Thankfully, at only three hours, their closing was short.

And so to the voting. We already knew Trump was acquitted under Senate counting rules, but anyone who followed the trial saw that it was Trump—just like the butler—who did it! But as any law professor will tell you—don't confuse a not-guilty verdict with justice.

Schumer Speaks after the Verdict

Following the votes, those senators who want to are allowed to speak. Typically, the Senate majority leader will speak first, followed by the Minority Leader; and that's how it played.

Chuck Schumer said the case was "open and shut." He said,

> Trump lied saying the election was stolen. He had laid the groundwork for this "big lie" in the months before the election. He told the big lie on election night, and he repeated the big

lie more than one hundred times in the weeks afterwards. He summoned his supporters to Washington, assembled them on the Ellipse, whipped them into a frenzy, and directed them at the Capitol.

Nothing Schumer said was unexpected. Talking about what happened, he said,

> None of the facts were up for debate. We saw it. We heard it. We lived it. This was the first presidential impeachment trial in history in which all Senators were not only judges and jurors but witnesses to the constitutional crime that was committed.

He was critical of the defence team, saying,

> Essentially, the president's counsel told the Senate that the Constitution was unconstitutional. Thankfully, the Senate took a firm stance and set a firm precedent, with a bipartisan vote, in favor of our power to try former officials for acts they committed while in office.

This was a reference to an earlier failed Republican motion that the trial was unconstitutional as Trump was no longer in office.

Like anyone with a brain, Schumer knew Trump was guilty of incitement and said,

> If President Trump hadn't told his supporters to march towards the Capitol, if he hadn't implored them to come to Washington on January 6 in the first place, if he hadn't repeatedly lied to them that the election was stolen and that their country was being taken from

them, the attack would not have happened, could not have happened.

He went on to say, "January 6 would not have happened but for the actions of Donald Trump." He was absolutely right.

Showing his disdain for those senators who voted to acquit, Schumer said,

> By not recognising the heinous crime that Donald Trump committed against the Constitution, Republican senators have not only risked but potentially invited the same danger that was just visited upon us. So let me say this: despite the results of the vote on Donald Trump's conviction in the court of impeachment, he deserves to be convicted— and I believe he will be convicted—in the court of public opinion.

It was all good, powerful stuff, just as you would expect, and Schumer closed by saying,

> Let the record show, before God, history, and the solemn oath we swear to the Constitution, that there was only one correct verdict in this trial: guilty. And I pray that while justice was not done in this trial, it will be carried forward by the American people, who above any of us in this chamber, determine the destiny of our great nation.

Now It's McConnell's Turn

McConnell had already confirmed in the morning he would be voting to acquit, so his remarks were unexpected.

He began by criticising the rioters, outlining some of their actions; but he blamed only one person, saying of the rioters, "They did this because they'd been fed wild falsehoods by the most powerful man on earth because he was angry he'd lost an election. Former President Trump's actions [that] preceded the riot were a disgraceful dereliction of duty."

He went on to say, "There's no question, none, that President Trump is practically and morally responsible for provoking the events of the day. No question about it." These were not the words we expected to hear from someone who voted to acquit.

Highlighting Trump's culpability, McConnell said, "The people who stormed this building believed they were acting on the wishes and instructions of their president, and having that belief was a foreseeable consequence of the growing crescendo of false statements, conspiracy theories, and reckless hyperbole, which the defeated president kept shouting into the largest megaphone on planet Earth."

He also touched on the prosecution's claim that Trump did nothing to stop the rioters despite calls he had received. McConnell simply said, "He did not do his job. He didn't take steps so federal law could be faithfully executed and order restored. No. Instead, according to public reports, he watched television happily as the chaos unfolded."

Now, this is all very well, but having effectively argued the prosecution case, he still voted to acquit. His argument was that the trial was unconstitutional because Trump was no longer president, but McConnell said when Trump was president, he would not accept delivery of the impeachment paper before inauguration day. Something of a "Catch-22" in that. Nice one, Mitch!

However, McConnell did suggest that Trump could still be pursued as a private citizen, saying, "We have a criminal justice system in this country. We have civil litigation. And former presidents are not immune from being held accountable by either one."

President Harry Truman (1945–1953) was famous for his "the buck stops here" phrase, but perhaps Slippery Mitch should be known for "the buck does not stop with the Senate when it doesn't suit my purposes, especially when we can pass the problem to someone else"—or something to that effect!

He had no hesitation in holding Trump responsible for the events of 6 January 2021, but by voting to acquit, he stayed with the party line. Criticising Trump is OK, but voting against him would have been a step too far. So it looks to me like Slippery may just have had his cake and eaten it too, but we don't need Einstein to tell us Trump will respond.

What Did We Learn from the Trial?

It was good that the trial was short, but it is important that we could all see exactly what happened and get those horrendous events into the record books. Biden can now get on with things.

However, the trial highlighted the divisions within the broader Republican Party and it is likely to be some time before there is any resolution to this. Trump is such a divisive character that it is a matter of love or hate; there is no in-between. Those that love him are loyal to the man; those that hate him just want him out. They see no place for "the party of Trump."

McConnell is looking to regain the Senate in the 2022 mid-term elections and blames Trump for losing those two critical senate seats in Georgia and thus the Senate in the last election. He is right, but Trump—of course—blames McConnell.

With this tension now out in the open, the behaviour of all Republican members of Congress will, for the foreseeable future, be viewed through the lens of the party's internecine war.

Even more reason to rip off the plaster and kick Trump and his family into political obscurity. Democrats too want to be rid of the beast, but they would be quite happy if he hangs around long enough to screw things up for Republicans at the midterms, ensuring they keep the Senate. But after that, it will be "on yer bike, matey!"

Thanks to McConnell's comments, concerns that Dodgy Don would boast about his acquittal seem remote, even though he will probably still claim the election was stolen. However, it doesn't really matter that Trump was acquitted because we have all seen how utterly self-obsessed and heartless he is, and he has definitely been found guilty in the court of public opinion.

With all those who have suffered, it can be only a matter of time before Trump deservedly faces prosecution. OK, let me dream!

My frustration is that Republican senators who have expressed privately they are against Trump did not band together and find him guilty. I understand their not wanting to find against him, but had they done so, their message to all state party members would have been crystal clear. And I'm sure they would have found safety in numbers. Easier said than done.

Kinzinger under Attack from Family

It came to light two days after the 6 January riot that eleven members of Congressman Adam Kinzinger's extended religious family were so upset he voted to impeach Trump that they sent him a letter, copied to "many conservative Republicans." It was penned by a cousin, Karen Otto.

The letter reflects the family's belief in God, their tolerance, their understanding, their wonderful Christian values, and their warmth. It begins, "Oh my, what a disappointment you are to us and to God! How do you call yourself a Christian when you join 'the devil's army,' believing in abortion!" WTF?

The letter is filled with references to God and the Bible, mentioning "the devil's army" several times. It calls for Kinzinger's resignation; and best of all, they write, "It is most embarrassing to us that we are related to you. You have embarrassed the Kinzinger family name!" Yeah, sure he has!

In a postscript, as if to confirm she is right, Otto proudly writes, "I have received numerous calls concerning your actions and egregious behavior towards our president of the United States of America, Donald J. Trump." I feel a salute coming on!

Kinzinger's reaction was pretty muted, saying only that his family were "misled."

The family, who clearly put the "zing" in Kinzinger, responded by writing a second letter on 19 January, again penned by Crazy Cousin Karen, saying, "Seriously, Adam, really! You are the one being misled [brainwashed] by the Democrats and the fake news media. Again, we thought you were 'smart enough' to realize they were manipulating your mind. We have not disowned you. You have disowned yourself."

Referring to his military service, Otto writes "As a member of the military, disrespecting your Commander-in-Chief is an act of Treason… To give up your Christian Principles for self-gain is deplorable."

The letter ends with a dig at House Speaker, Nancy Pelosi "Perhaps the witch/devil, holding the gavel, will invite you to her house for ice-cream". Wow!

With all this fire-and-brimstone stuff, both letters are quite disturbing; and it seems that, for this group of crazies, the words 'God' and 'Trump' are interchangeable.

Funny to think that Kinzinger was brought up in a town called Normal, Illinois! Presumably cousin Karen wasn't!

Trump and Giuliani Accused of Conspiring to Incite Capitol Riot

Surprise! Surprise! Only three days after Trump was acquitted by the Senate on his second impeachment charge, Democratic congressman Bennie Thompson from Mississippi and the civil rights organisation, the NAACP,[21] bring a lawsuit against Trump and Giuliani, together with the Proud Boys and Oath Keepers, accusing them of conspiring to incite the 6 January attack on the Capitol.

They argue that Trump and the rest violated a post-Civil War act known as the Ku Klux Klan Act passed in 1871 to combat violence by the KKK, allowing Black people to take action against hate groups who use "force, intimidation, or threat" to prevent any-

---

[21] National Association for the Advancement of Colored People.

one from upholding the duties of their office. It's ironic that a 150-year-old law aimed at protecting the Black community can be used against Trump.

Thompson said he brought the suit because Trump's "gleeful support of violent White supremacists led to a breach of the Capitol that put my life, and that of my colleagues, in grave danger."

Sadly, we will not see a resolution to this case for some time as this is just another of the many cases Trump faces and will face long into the future. At least someone is trying to hold Trump accountable.

Trump Attacks McConnell

On the same day that Trump is named in the Ku Klux Klan case, he predictably responds to Mitch McConnell's post-trial speech and launches a scathing attack on him, saying, "Mitch is a dour, sullen, and unsmiling political hack, and if Republican senators are going to stay with him, they will not win again."

He adds, "The Republican Party can never again be respected or strong with political 'leaders' like Senator Mitch McConnell at its helm."

Criticising him in as many ways as he could, Trump said, "McConnell's dedication to business as usual, status quo policies—together with his lack of political insight, wisdom, skill, and personality—has rapidly driven him from majority leader to minority leader, and it will only get worse."

He also suggested that the Democrats had McConnell in their pockets with the taunt "The Democrats and Chuck Schumer play McConnell like a fiddle—they've never had it so good—and they want to keep it that way!"

All good childish stuff, especially as there are reports that Trump had originally written that McConnell had "too many chins but not enough smarts" but was persuaded to remove it.

Texas in Winter Storm, but Ted Cruz Shines

Now for a change of scenery.

As winter storms sweep across the US, Texas suffers rare prolonged sub-zero temperatures. February temperatures in Texas average a high of 16°C (61°F) and a low of 5°C (41°F), but on 16 February, Dallas-Fort Worth International Airport recorded its coldest temperatures in seventy-two years at -19°C (-2°F).

Throughout the state, more than four million homes and businesses lost power and water, many for several days; and before some sense of normality was resumed, the weather accounted for thirty-two lives.

Republican Texas governor Greg Abbott, critic of the Green New Deal—a congressional resolution laying out a plan for tackling climate change—initially blamed renewable energy sources for the power outages, citing frozen wind turbines as an example of their unreliability.

However, less than a quarter of the state's energy comes from renewable sources; most comes from natural-gas-powered generating facilities, which either froze or suffered mechanical failures. Abbott later fell in line with the truth, albeit somewhat reluctantly.

Given the circumstances, you might imagine that a senator of your state would stick around to see how he or she could help or stay just to show solidarity with everyone else.

Well, if you thought that of Tosser Ted, you'd have been wrong! So what did Ted do when millions were freezing in their Texas homes? He went to Mexico—Cancún, to be precise!

He tried to sneak away unnoticed but was seen and photographed at the airport. Gotcha! So with his tail between his legs, Tainted Ted came back the next day and said his daughters, aged ten and twelve, who were off school for a week, had suggested the break; and Ted, "to be a good dad," said OK. I love the fact Ted is such a "good dad" that he blames his daughters. What a class act!

Anyway, Truthful Ted tells us that together with his wife, he went on the trip to make sure they got there safely. Of course you did! Later on, when he realised this story was not going away,

Not-So-Truthful Ted said, "From the moment I sat on the plane, I began second-guessing that decision." Love 'im to bits!

But then the real truth finally came out. It was his wife, not his daughters, who suggested the getaway! She texted friends, saying they were "freezing" at home, having been without heat or power for two days.

So finally, Tattered Ted admits he was wrong, telling reporters, "On the one hand, all of us who are parents have a responsibility to take care of our kids, take care of our families."

But then, in full-on Creepy Cruz mode, he says, "But I also have a responsibility that I take very seriously of fighting for the state of Texas. As it became a bigger and bigger firestorm, it became all the more compelling that I needed to come back."

What utter bollocks! The only reason you went back was because you got caught trying to get away. I can almost hear the people of Texas echoing the words of Adam Kinzinger's crazy cousin, saying to Teddy boy, "Oh my, what a disappointment you are to us and to God!"

Biden Marks Five Hundred Thousand US Lives Lost to COVID-19

On Monday, 22 February, just three days after the US recorded twenty-eight million coronavirus cases, Joe Biden commemorates the loss of half a million American lives to COVID-19.

Standing in front of the White House North Lawn with his wife Jill and Kamala Harris and her husband, the "second gentleman" Doug Emhoff, he gives a short speech capturing the mood of the moment, saying, "Today, we mark a truly grim, heartbreaking milestone—500,071 dead. That's more Americans who died in one year in this pandemic than in World War I, World War II, and the Vietnam War combined."

He says that both for individuals and for the nation, "remembrance" is an important part of the healing process.

Five hundred candles had been placed on the steps leading down to the South Lawn; and addressing those who have lost loved ones, he says, "They're never truly gone. They'll always be part of your heart." Biden does what needs to be done and says what needs to be said. It's good to see the US with a real president again.

How the Mighty Might Have Fallen

It comes as a shock to learn that New York state governor Andrew Cuomo is accused of under-reporting nursing-home deaths in New York state. Later, there is criticism of his authoritarian, bullying style of management, and then a few days later, he is accused of sexual harassment by two of his former aides.

An end-of-January report by New York state's attorney general Letitia James's investigators finds that nursing-home deaths in New York may have been under-reported by as much as 50 percent. Cuomo denies he fudged the numbers, claiming the total number of deaths was accurately reported, but as we move into February, the story gets a lot more traction.

The accusation against Cuomo is that the 8,500 reported care-home deaths should have been reported as 15,000 because the deaths were reported being at the place of death rather than the deceased's registered address—namely, the nursing home.

Although Cuomo acknowledges the delay in reporting the higher numbers, he claims he didn't want the numbers to be double-counted, but one of his former aides said the governor delayed release of the data as he thought Trump would "turn it into a political football."

Cuomo is certainly under pressure as the US Attorney's office in Brooklyn and the FBI are looking at data surrounding COVID-19 deaths.

Another accusation comes from Assemblyman Ron Kim, who criticised Cuomo over his handling of care-home COVID-related deaths, saying Cuomo threatened to destroy his career. Kim said Cuomo was "berating, yelling, and threatening that I have to issue a statement that invalidated what I heard."

New York City's mayor, Bill de Blasio, who is definitely no friend of Cuomo, says, "This is classic Andrew Cuomo. The bullying is nothing new."

And it doesn't stop there—Lindsey Boylan, a former aide to Cuomo and an economic adviser in his administration, said in a tweet at the end of last year that Cuomo "sexually harassed me for years." Then in late February, she publishes an essay detailing further claims.

She accuses the New York governor of going "out of his way to touch me on my lower back, arms, and legs." She also accused him of once kissing her on the lips and asking her to play strip poker while on his private jet. Others on the jet deny the claim.

There are other accusations, but a spokesperson for Cuomo says, referring to an earlier denial on 24 February, "As we said before, Ms. Boylan's claims of inappropriate behaviour are quite simply false." Boylan worked with Cuomo for three years.

It's difficult to understand the gravity of Governor Cuomo's situation. Since last summer, nine of his top health officials have resigned, many attributing their decision directly to Cuomo's changing pandemic policies that they learned about from press conferences. Others resigned due to his changes to the vaccination programme.

Whatever the reasons, clearly he is not running a happy ship, and many are critical of his management style. When asked about this at the end of January, he said, "When I say 'experts' in air quotes, it sounds like I'm saying I don't really trust the experts—because I don't."

Thinking we are looking at one sexual harassment accusation, we learn of a second as a twenty-five-year-old former aide, Charlotte Bennett, says that in conversations with Cuomo in June last year, he told her he was open to dating women in their twenties and asked her if she was monogamous and had ever had sex with older men. She says Cuomo asked her a number of personal questions but never touched her.

However, she said, "I understood that the governor wanted to sleep with me and felt horribly uncomfortable and scared." She reported the conversations to his chief of staff and was moved to another position within the administration. Bennett said she decided not to insist on an investigation because she was happy in her new job and "wanted to move on."

On Saturday, 27 February, Cuomo admits to asking Bennett personal questions but denies the allegations, saying in a statement that he believed he had been acting as a mentor and had "never made advances toward Ms. Bennett, nor did I ever intend to act in any way that was inappropriate." Cuomo has requested an "outside review" of the matter and hopes that people await the findings "before making any judgments."

Accusations of fudging coronavirus numbers or office bullying are serious enough, but when it comes to sexual harassment, we are in completely different territory. This is a land mine of a subject.

Too often, accusations against men boil down to "her word against his." And perhaps too often, "his" word is the one accepted. A sad fact is that rarely are these cases cut-and-dried, and that is why the outcome is so often disappointing.

It's ironic to see someone who was so impressive at the height of the pandemic and who displayed such leadership is now facing calls for him to resign.

I make no judgement of Cuomo, but no matter what, he is not in a good place.

Moving into March, we learn of more accusers of sexual harassment. This story is by no means over.

March 2021

Johnson & Johnson Get the Go-Ahead on One-Shot Vaccines

This time last year, the US recorded its first COVID-19 death, but one year later, the month gets off to a completely different start. Over the weekend, the FDA and CDC gave the green light for emergency use of J&J's vaccine; and today, Monday, 1 March, deliveries of four million vaccines begins.

So the US will now have three vaccines in circulation, but J&J's offering is different as only one dose is required. One and done! J&J plans to deliver twenty million doses by the end of March and one hundred million by summer. This gives real hope that by the end of summer or early autumn, herd immunity will be reached.

COVID Cases Tumble… But

Coronavirus cases currently average mid-sixty thousands, compared with those crazy early January days when case numbers peaked at over three hundred thousand a day. Of course, this is news to be celebrated, but Biden's coronavirus team warns about complacency, especially in light of the new variants.

There are real fears that the new variants may cause another spike in cases. The UK variant is currently doubling its share of US cases every ten days or so and currently accounts for an estimated 20 percent of all US cases.

Whilst the fall in numbers is great news, case numbers have held stable in the last three weeks, prompting Dr. Anthony Fauci to say, "We're plateauing at quite a high level—sixty to seventy thousand new infections per day is quite high."

He said the best way to prevent further spread is to "get people vaccinated as quickly and as expeditiously as possible and, above all, maintain the public health measures that we talk about so often."

Having done so well, the last thing we need is another coronavirus surge. We need a vaccination surge instead!

Meghan and Harry Light a Fire under the Royal Family

Yesterday, at 9:00 p.m., Sunday, 7 March, an Oprah Winfrey interview with Meghan Markel, Duchess of Sussex, and her husband Prince Harry was aired on US television. I mention it not to remark on the comments, criticisms, and accusations made by the couple but simply to record when it happened.

From the moment it was broadcast, it became indelibly written into the history of the British royal family and will doubtless be forever compared with the equally explosive interview given by Harry's mother Princess Diana in November 1995, three years after her separation from Prince Charles in December 1992.

President Biden Wins Approval of $1.9 Trillion Aid Package

After much debate and gnashing of teeth, Biden's COVID rescue package passed the Senate, voting fifty to forty-nine, and he signed it into law on Thursday, 11 March.

A good result, giving much needed help, but I suppose we shouldn't be surprised that no Republican senators voted in support of the package—this despite 70 percent of Republicans polled in the general population were in support of Biden's proposal.

The bill is wide-ranging and includes direct payments of up to $1,400 to nearly 160 million Americans, a $300 weekly boost to jobless benefits through September, and a one-year expansion of the child tax.

It earmarks $130 billion for the opening of schools. In the health sector, it puts $20 billion into a national vaccine programme, $50 billion to expand testing capabilities, $30 billion for increasing the supply of PPE, and more. US airlines also benefit from $14 billion in payroll support and $1 billion for airline contractors.

How ironic it is that Trump's $2 trillion package one year ago achieved full Democratic support (ninety-six to zero), but not one single Republican sided with Biden this time. Disappointing, to say the least. And so much for McConnell's lovey-dovey comment last year when he got Democratic support, saying, "I think it says a lot about the United States Senate as an institution, our willingness to put aside our differences and to do something really significant for the country."

So Slippery Mitch is fine setting aside political differences when he needs the Democrats but rediscovers them when he thinks he may be able to screw the Dems over!

But don't be too hard on him—he's only a politician.

Does the Senate Need a Makeover?

At election time, I touched on the Electoral College system and showed how, in some ways, it is flawed; but with Biden's stimulus package just squeaking through the Senate with the slimmest of margins, perhaps there should be discussion on the structure of the Senate given how widely popular the package was with the general public.

Let's take a quick look at a bit of history.

The structure of the Houses of Congress was decided at the Constitutional Convention of 1787, coming about as a result the of the so-called "Great Compromise" between large and small states. It was ratified in 1788 and implemented in 1789, at which time there were thirteen states, resulting in twenty-six senators and sixty-five representatives. The population of the country at that time was a mere four million.

When the number in the House of Representatives was capped at 435 in 1929, the population of the country was 122 million and today stands at 330 million. That is why I ask if the Senate needs a makeover.

The House of Representatives, notwithstanding gerrymandering issues, better lends itself to reaching bipartisan agreement, but I'm not sure if the Senate today adequately represents the will of the people. I say it doesn't and given the population growth, there is an argument that would call for an increase in the number of senators in the larger states.

California, the most populous state in the country (39.4 million) with its two senators, has the same population as the twenty-one least-populated states combined, with their forty-two senators.

We already know that if the last two Senate seats in Georgia had gone to Republicans in the last election, they would have a fifty-two to forty-eight Senate majority, meaning Biden would not be able to make good on the very promises that got him elected.

Surely, winning the popular vote by eight million should give any president an easier ride than that which Biden is getting.

Looking at it from another perspective, today's 50 Democratic senators represent 184 million Americans, compared with 146 million represented by Republican senators—a difference of 38 million or more than 11 percent of the population.

Needless to say, nothing will change for a long time - if ever - as the only thing politicians can agree on is the time; but at some point, I think either the Electoral College or the structure of Congress, or both, will have to change.

Just look at the Senate and the way it votes. Today some matters need a simple majority to pass in the Senate, some sixty votes, and others a so-called super majority of sixty-seven votes!

All this does is give senators the opportunity to play silly buggers and be king or queen for a day, especially when majorities are thin.

So why not increase the number of senators to be more representative of the populations they serve and have all decisions voted on the basis of a simple majority? Maybe even abolish the Senate altogether and beef up the House of Representatives? Too radical? Too simple? Maybe, but as things stand, the Senate holds too much sway.

John Magufuli, President of Tanzania

What? How is the president of Tanzania relevant? Well, President John Pombe Joseph Magufuli is dead. He was a staunch COVID skeptic, an autocratic leader who believed vaccines were a conspiracy against Africans and was a through-and-through fruit-cake—not too unlike someone orange we know.

In April last year, as a means of ridding the country of COVID, he urged everybody to go to church and called for three days of national prayer, declaring "the satanic virus cannot live in the body of Jesus Christ." So in May, Tanzania stopped publishing figures of COVID cases, and in June, he claimed his country had eradicated coronavirus "by the grace of God." So presumably the prayers worked!

Instead of vaccines, Magufuli favoured the use of herbal medicine and steam treatments; but sadly for him, despite munching on holy basil in his sauna, he became ill at the end of February and died less than three weeks later. It is widely believed he had COVID, but a heart attack was given as the cause of death for this healthy-looking sixty-one-year-old.

Magufuli's main political rival, Tundu Lissu, said,

> This is a president whose denial of COVID-19, whose attempts to cover it up, whose adamant refusal to take any action to combat the pandemic, who has thumbed his nose to the world, refused any international or regional cooperation to deal with COVID-19 and now he goes down with COVID-19—that is poetic justice to me.

Magufuli truly was a raving nutter. Last year, apart from his three days of prayer nonsense, he blamed the number of cases on fake positive tests; so to prove his case, he arranged for samples from a goat, a sheep, a bird, and a papaya to be taken and sent for testing. The samples were given human names, and the papaya tested positive. It was probably called Donald.

Trump Gets the Vaccine

We learn that One-Term and his wife have been vaccinated—back in January! It seems they did it very privately before leaving the White House. Presumably, Dodgy didn't want his base to know. But now, the cat's out of the bag, and he's under pressure to encourage everyone to follow his example.

The vaccine has its doubters and refusers who span the full political spectrum, but surveys show that men who identify as Republican are in the majority. However, to his credit, on 17 March, Dodgy Don said on Fox, "I would recommend it, and I would recommend it to a lot of people that don't want to get it. And a lot of those people voted for me, frankly."

It was good that he said that; but just as you thought he was being responsible, he added, "But again, we have our freedoms, and we have to live by that. And I agree with that also. But it is a great vaccine. It is a safe vaccine, and it is something that works." So he recommends it but can't stop himself from diluting the message.

A CNN poll shows 92 percent of Democrats have either been vaccinated or want to get vaccinated, compared with 50 percent of Republicans. I'm sure that will change as more people get their vaccinations, especially when we see an easing in restrictions and the new variants are causing large spikes in cases in Florida and Michigan.

Exceptions, however, are likely to be White evangelicals, according to *The New York Times*, which reports that their refusal to take the vaccine could prolong the pandemic.

But some of these people live in worlds of their own. A minister in Washington state said he received a divine message that God was the ultimate healer and deliverer and that "the vaccine is not the savior." Another crazy example is an Oklahoma woman who refuses the vaccine because she believes it contains aborted cell tissue. WTF?

The NYT says there are about forty-one million White evangelical adults in the US, about 45 percent of whom said in late February that they would not get vaccinated. But why? The answer appears largely to be religious faith in combination with a wariness of mainstream science, general distrust and conspiracy theories.

This is so frustrating, because when it comes to the vaccination, these people rely on their faith, but when they're ill, they rely on their doctors.

Chaos at the Border

On taking office, among the first actions President Biden took was to sign a raft of executive orders reversing a number of Trump's immigration policies and putting in place a reform bill giving a path to citizenship for undocumented individuals.

This is unquestionably good news, but taking all things together, his actions were seen as a relaxation of all border restrictions. And the result is massive numbers of migrants arriving at the border, looking to start a new life in the US.

In particular, the number of unaccompanied children has skyrocketed to fourteen thousand, many of whom have come to the US to reunite with family members and others to escape violence and poverty in their home countries.

Biden's team have been chasing around, trying to find suitable accommodation for the children, and according to reports, Biden thinks the process is taking too long. Maybe so, but it also looks like this wasn't thought through terribly well in the first place. And to make matters worse, there are reports that say Biden was cautioned early on against this happening. Not good. And in the meantime, the children continue to live in inadequate overcrowded conditions.

Understandably, Republicans, many of whom criticised Biden's early executive orders, have been enjoying his discomfort with "I told you sos" being thrown around left and right, but the fact is they are right. Biden has got off to a great start, but his handling of this crisis is definitely not his finest hour.

An unnamed Homeland Security official described Biden's problems as being "self-inflicted," which seems pretty accurate. Biden has charged VP Harris with the task of resolving this problem, which others describe as a crisis.

I'm hopeful that the problems can be resolved, but there is no quick fix here.

Biden Announces Massive Infrastructure Plan

Biden is not hanging around. On the last day of the month, he announces his nearly $2.3 trillion eight-year infrastructure plan, which he labels the American Jobs Plan, to be paid for by increasing the corporate tax rate from 21 percent to 28 percent over fifteen years. The main highlights of the plan are

- $650 billion for physical infrastructure
- $300 billion for housing infrastructure
- $300 billion for manufacturing.
- $300 billion for electric grid.
- $400 billion for home caretakers, care for the elderly and disabled.

Needless to say, Republicans are all against it, and for that matter, not all Democrats are on board. There's no way Biden will succeed with everything he wants, but it will be a test to see if he can get anything agreed on a bipartisan basis.

April 2021

Mass Shootings Again in the News

We start the month with news of another mass shooting. A mass shooting in the US is widely defined as whenever four or more people are shot (injured or killed), not including the shooter(s). Well, today, the first day of April, we learn of four people, including one child, being shot and killed in Orange, California.

Two weeks ago, we learned of a mass shooting in Atlanta, Georgia, where a twenty-one-year-old man walked into a grocery shop and killed ten people. Two days later, there was another mass shooting, this time in Boulder, Colorado, where another twenty-one-year-old killed eight people, six of whom were Asian women, at three separate locations. Both gunmen were captured alive and taken into custody.

Today's shooting is not the third but the twentieth mass shooting in the last two weeks. Yes, the twentieth mass shooting in two weeks! What on earth is wrong with people?

I need hardly mention that these events again spark discussions on gun control and background checks. Politicians condemn the acts of these murderers. They express horror and outrage, offer their thoughts and prayers, and then do nothing.

Some politicians, especially those who receive funding from the National Rifle Association (NRA), strongly oppose changes to the laws on guns and actually advocate for more guns, quoting the NRA mantra: "The only thing that stops a bad guy with a gun is a good guy with a gun." But they're wrong.

They wouldn't need good guys with guns if they stopped guns being given to bad guys in the first place. They're bloody idiots!

According to a 2018 report, the Geneva-based Small Arms Survey found that the United States, with its 330 million population, has nearly 400 million guns in the hands of private citizens—by far more, numerically and per capita, than any other country in the world.

By the end of April, more than fifty mass shootings in the month are recorded with thirty-three dead and 210 injured.

Capitol Policeman Killed Near Capitol Building

On Friday, 2 April, a twenty-five-year-old man drove his car at two Capitol police officers, hitting them both and then crashing into a concrete barrier. He then got out of the car, armed with a knife, and ran at a third officer who shot and killed him.

One of the two officers hit by the car, Officer William "Billy" Evans, who had been with the force for eighteen years, died of injuries sustained. The second officer was admitted to hospital and released a few days later.

Concerns were expressed that the attacker may have been from a far-right group, but this turned out not to be the case. He was suffering from delusions, paranoia, and suicidal thoughts, according to reports; and investigators are viewing it as an isolated incident. What a pointless loss of two lives.

Matt Gaetz—What a Lowlife

I touched briefly on Florida representative Matt Gaetz when looking at crazies in the Republican Party. I described him as a nutter; but I should have added that he is also a sad, juvenile, self-publicising, inadequate, attention-craving Trump fanatic with zero emotional intelligence. And those are just his positive qualities!

A good example of his cretinous behaviour is when, to show he was against mask-wearing, wore a gas mask before voting on a coronavirus bill at the beginning of the pandemic. He certainly got the attention he wanted; and his constant praising of Trump earned him plenty of airtime on Fox, where has reportedly made 180 appearances.

However, despite his being a nobody, we should take a look at him. This sleazebag, who has shown pictures to colleagues on the floor of the House of naked women he apparently paid to have sex with, is being investigated for having sex with a minor. Oh yes, and he is also under a federal investigation into possible sex-trafficking violations. What a charmer!

Following the accusations, he was interviewed on Fox by Tucker Carlson, another total lowlife, to discuss the investigation; and what a weird interview it was, as it showed that fact really can be stranger than fiction. Gaetz denied the accusations but was more interested in talking about a former Department of Justice official, David McGee, who was trying to extort $25 million from his father, and that his father had been asked by the FBI to wear a wire for a second time at a meeting with a coconspirator of McGee's. What?

Gaetz said if the money was paid, McGee could then make the investigation into him "go away." So there was the link—if the father paid up, the investigation into his son would magically go away.

It was totally confusing as Gaetz was not at all clear about time lines or people and was not convincing. Carlson said afterwards that this was "one of the weirdest interviews" he'd ever conducted.

However, somewhat surprisingly, Gaetz's father, a former senator for Florida, later confirmed he had indeed been approached! He had met with an ex-air force intelligence officer, Bob Kent, who told him his son was having "legal issues" and that the funds were needed to pay for an effort to free someone called Robert Levinson, a former FBI agent who disappeared in Iran in 2007.

Kent claimed he has video evidence that Levinson was still alive and being held hostage, despite reports of his death. This is seriously weird stuff.

And if this is not confusing enough already, on Tuesday, 6 April, a week after the Fox interview, *The New York Times* reports that in the months before Trump left office, Gaetz asked One-Term for a "preemptive blanket pardon." This request came when Trump's Department of Justice were investigating whether he had sex with a minor.

Despite the pressure he's under, Gaetz refuses to resign but says, "My lifestyle of yesteryear may be different from how I live now, but it was not and is not illegal." So it appears he may not be denying paying for sex but does deny having sex with a minor.

At this point, you need to know of another player in this farce; and that is Gaetz's friend, Joel Greenberg, who was arrested in June 2020 on twelve charges, also including sex trafficking of a child, as well as stalking and aggravated identity theft. He's allowed bail, but the dipstick violates the terms and is arrested again on 3 March 2021 and is to remain behind bars until his trial.

On 31 March, Greenberg faces twenty-one additional charges, including charges related to cryptocurrency fraud and special business administration loan fraud; and it is around this time we learn of the close friendship between Gaetz and Greenberg. It just gets better all the time.

But sadly, the Gaetz story will not be over before the end of my book, so I will miss out on writing about the fate of this sleazeball.

However, in May, we discover that his buddy, Joel Greenberg, enters into a plea agreement, pleading guilty to six out of an original thirty-three charges They are sex trafficking of a child, production of a false document, aggravated identity theft, wire fraud, stalking, and conspiracy to commit an offense against the US.

As part of that deal, the federal government will dismiss the other twenty-seven charges in exchange for Greenberg's cooperation in the investigation and prosecution of others. His cooperation also includes disclosing any evidence or relevant information to the investigation.

Even better, in late May, Gaetz's ex-girlfriend agrees to help prosecutors. Oh, and for good measure, his buddy Greenberg says Gaetz did have sex with a minor.

It is hard to believe Gaetz is not up to his neck in it. People like him have no place decent society—but nor does Trump. And that's probably why they get on so well!

Prince Philip, Duke of Edinburgh—10 June 1921–9 April 2021

Prince Philip, husband of seventy-three years to Queen Elizabeth II, was laid to rest at Windsor on Saturday, 17 April 2021, just two months before what would have been his one hundredth birthday. The funeral was low-key, and due to COVID-19 restrictions, only thirty family members were in attendance instead of what would normally have been eight hundred. Ironically, on that same day, the number of COVID-19 cases recorded worldwide topped thirty million.

Just as COVID-19 had impacted the funeral, it impacted the last year of Philip's life. Prince Philip, who retired from royal duties at age ninety-six, spent the last year together with the queen at Windsor, who, because of COVID-19, cancelled all her engagements. So they were together all that time—the longest period in all their marriage.

The funeral was modest and very touching; it was a simple family service. Perhaps, most poignant was seeing the queen sitting alone with her head bowed as she followed proceedings; and perhaps Prince Philip's influence to effect a reconciliation between two of his grandsons, Harry and William, was in evidence as we saw them walk together after the funeral.

George Floyd: The Trial of Derek Chauvin

Chauvin's trial took place at Hennepin County Government Center in Minneapolis, Minnesota; and for the first time, thanks to the pandemic and a decision by the presiding judge, Judge Peter

Cahill, it was televised. The decision was made despite objections by the prosecution, who felt televising the trial may intimidate some witnesses. No images of the jury were to be shown.

With the trial starting on Monday, 29 March, the prosecution and defence had rested their cases by Thursday, 15 April; and Monday, 19 April, was the date set for closing arguments.

It was decided that Chauvin was to be charged separately from the other officers involved in Floyd's arrest and death. He faced three charges:

- *Second-degree unintentional murder.* To convict, the prosecutors must show beyond a reasonable doubt that Chauvin caused Floyd's death while assaulting him, but they do not have to show Chauvin caused his death intentionally. Sentence—maximum of forty years.
- *Third-degree murder.* Requires the prosecutors to prove that Chauvin caused Floyd's death "by perpetrating an act eminently dangerous to others and evincing a depraved mind, without regard for human life." Sentence—maximum of twenty-five years.
- *Second-degree murder.* Here, the prosecutors need to prove Chauvin caused Floyd's death by "culpable negligence whereby the person creates an unreasonable risk and consciously takes chances of causing death or great bodily harm." Sentence—maximum of ten years.

If guilty on all three charges, it would not mean aggregating all the sentences. Instead, Chauvin could expect to be convicted of the most serious offense, but the situation is complicated by the fact that he has no previous convictions and, under Minnesota sentencing guidelines, would face shorter sentences—twelve and a half years, twelve and a half years, and four years for each of the cases, respectively.

However, this brings into play "aggravating factors," where the prosecution can argue for higher sentences.

As the trial began, one of the first things we learned was that George Floyd was under Chauvin's knee for nine minutes and twenty-nine seconds, not eight minutes and forty-six seconds as had previously been measured, and that the full event had been recorded on a mobile phone of Darnella Frazier, a teenager who was seventeen years old at the time.

The prosecution played her recording in its entirety, and we were to discover that nine minutes and twenty-nine seconds is a long, long time. It was very distressing to watch yet extremely impactful and was one of the key pieces of evidence in the case against Chauvin.

In total, the prosecution brought thirty-eight witnesses, including Floyd's girlfriend; one of his brothers, Philonise; various bystanders; as well as expert witnesses. All shared their story, and with each one, the case against Chauvin only grew stronger.

Among the most memorable witnesses were first a bystander and mixed martial arts fighter, Donald Wynn Williams II, who can be heard repeatedly asking Chauvin to check George Floyd's pulse, but to no avail. Through his eyes, we became witnesses to Floyd's death ourselves.

The second is head of the Minneapolis Police Department, Chief Medaria Arradondo, who was unequivocal in his criticism of Chauvin, saying, "To continue to apply that level of force to a person proned out [sic], handcuffed behind their back—that in no way, shape, or form is anything that is by policy," adding, "It is not part of our training, and it is certainly not part of our ethics or our values."

Two other police officers also testified against Chauvin, showing, for once, there was no "blue wall" of protection here.

However, the most memorable prosecution witness was a soft-spoken Irishman by the name of Dr. Martin Tobin, a pulmonologist and critical care doctor who explained the physiology of breathing. He was mesmerising and made complicated science accessible to all.

He took us through each stage of Floyd's suffering, explaining what was happening to Floyd's body, starting from the moment he was pinned down right through to the moment George Floyd took his last breath. It was utterly compelling.

After eleven days, the prosecution rested its case.

The case for the defence did not follow a central theme but instead was loosely based around Floyd's health and his history of drug use. He was reportedly "high" at the time, so could that have influenced his behaviour and therefore that of the police? They tried to argue that his enlarged heart may have been a contributory factor.

They tried unsuccessfully to pick holes in the testimony of Dr. Tobin and faced the problem of having to overcome part of Tobin's earlier testimony when he summed everything up in what was akin to a QED moment, saying, "A healthy person subjected to what Mr. Floyd was subjected to would have died." It was that simple.

It was not easy for the defence. They suggested carbon monoxide from the car exhaust may have played a role in his death. Strangest of all was they tried to prove Chauvin's actions had been fully in line with his training!

They were grabbing at straws; and even their own medical expert and final witness, Dr. David Fowler, was unconvincing. He testified that Floyd's death should be classified as undetermined due to underlying health conditions, and he claimed that Chauvin's knee on Floyd's neck was "not a significant factor in is death."

And it was Fowler who said that carbon monoxide may have played a role in George Floyd's death, resulting in the prosecution recalling Dr. Tobin as a rebuttal witness. Tobin testified that such an assertion was "simply wrong."

The defence had a bad hand from the start, and every new card they were dealt was worse than the last. They did what they could and rested their case after two days.

The closing arguments served only to reinforce what we already believed. The prosecution concentrated on the nine minutes and twenty-nine seconds; and the defence argued that those nine minutes and twenty-nine seconds should be looked at in the "context of the totality of the circumstances," referring to the preceding sixteen minutes and fifty-nine seconds, and argued Floyd died of heart disease and illegal drug use.

However, in rebuttal, Jerry Blackwell, for the prosecution, said, "You were told that Mr. Floyd died because his heart was too big. The truth of the matter is that the reason George Floyd is dead is because Mr. Chauvin's heart was too small."

At the end of closing arguments, Chauvin waived his right to have the jury rule on the aggravating factors, putting the decision on sentencing in the hands of Judge Cahill.

It looked clear Chauvin was guilty, but which way would the jury go? Any guilty verdict would have to be unanimous, and history was on Chauvin's side. As the trial was finishing, shops and businesses were boarding up their fronts in case of a not guilty verdict, and additional police had been drafted in, as had been the National Guard.

The jury took ten and a half hours to reach its verdict. The judge read out the charges one by one, and as he did, Chauvin looked anxiously about the court. He tried not to show his emotions, but he looked scared. And it was uncomfortable to watch. Guilty on all three charges! Unbelievable.

Chauvin stood, had his hands cuffed behind his back, and, after exchanging a word with his attorney, was led out of the courtroom. It was a powerful image and saddening to realise that none of this would have happened only if Chauvin had shown some basic compassion to George Floyd.

Instead of tears of frustration, there were tears of joy; and instead of riots in the streets, there were celebrations. We have just witnessed another never-to-be-forgotten day in American history.

We will learn in late June that Judge Peter Cahill sentences Chauvin to twenty-two and a half years in prison.

May 2021

COVID—Getting Better in the US but Not in India

We begin May with spring in the air and a spring in our step. COVID cases in the US are coming down. All states, bar two or three, are showing a decline in cases; and more importantly, hospitalisations and deaths are falling.

The month starts with cases at a daily average of 50,000 and will end at an average of 20,000—a tremendous result. The CDC says all fully vaccinated people no longer need to wear a mask outside; and Mayor de Blasio just announced that as of 1 July, New York will be fully open. Yes, fully open! So maybe at last, we are seeing the beginning of the end.

After a slow start, New York took good control of vaccinating its people, and as someone who is fully jabbed up, I am enjoying a feeling of great liberation! Still, 1 July is still some way off, but at least I don't have to wear a mask outside anymore.

Whilst we can hope to be over the worst, we are not out of the woods just yet. Vaccine hesitancy unexpectedly persists in some areas, but the Biden administration aims to have 70 percent of the population with at least one vaccination by 4 July.

But news from India is not good. After a successful period of control, the growth in cases has literally exploded over the last six weeks. Hospitals are overwhelmed, and there are multiple reports of people dying while waiting in line to be seen by a doctor.

Deaths in India are currently reported at 240,000 with cases of 22 million, but these numbers are not considered reliable. And reality is likely far worse. At the moment, India is reporting a staggering 400,000 cases and 4,000 deaths each day. Many countries are sending vaccines, but with a population of 1.4 billion, there is a long road ahead.

But there may be some cause for hope as even here, we will see the daily average for new cases falling from a midmonth high of 390,000 to 155,000 at the end of the month and still falling.

Maybe someone should start developing an oral vaccine.

The Price of Integrity in Politics

It is rare for the words *integrity* and *politicians* to be used positively in the same sentence—certainly not in the cases of Loser Lyndsey and Tosser Ted. And let's not forget Slippery Mitch and Whacky Kevin McCarthy. When you are with any one of these four, you are in a scruples-free zone.

There is nothing they won't do to advance themselves or to dump on someone else. They have forgotten that they swore an oath to "support and defend the Constitution of the United States against all enemies, foreign and domestic." They also swore to "well and faithfully discharge the duties of the office on which I am about to enter."

Of course, it's all rubbish because what they're really saying is "I solemnly swear I will do whatever it takes to gain or regain power and do whatever it takes to get elected or reelected."

But what about those few politicians who really do have integrity? Well, for the most part, they are likely to live their political lives on the fringes —at least in today's world they are.

Just look at all those who had the courage to denounce Trump's "big lie." Look at those in the House who voted to impeach Trump. Look at the likes of Adam Kinzinger and Elizabeth Cheney. All were censured by their own party, and we see later in the month Cheney is removed from her position of the third most senior Republican in the House of Representatives for being critical of Tin-Pot Trump.

At the beginning of the month, Trump, with increasing delusions of grandeur, had issued what he no doubt saw as a proclamation, saying, "The Fraudulent Presidential Election of 2020 will be, from this day forth, known as *the big lie!*" What an absolute tit! I'm surprised he didn't start with "Hear ye! Hear ye!"

It was Cheney's response that got her back into hot Republican water. She tweeted, "The 2020 presidential election was not stolen. Anyone who claims it was is spreading THE BIG LIE, turning their back on the rule of law, and poisoning our democratic system." A little over a week later, she was "given the elbow."

So sad to say, it's the unscrupulous who tend to succeed ahead of those with integrity. And right now, Slippery Mitch and Whacky Macky have their eyes on being, respectively, Senate majority leader and Speaker of the House after the 2022 midterm elections—and that's all that matters!

So What About the Midterms?

Despite the fact Biden has hardly had a chance to warm his presidential seat, many pundits are already saying the Republicans are well placed to regain the House and the Senate at the midterm! What?

But the fact is that if Republicans are successful, Biden's plans may remain nothing more than plans as his presidency will likely be doomed to failure.

With the prize of regaining power, Slippery and Whacky are therefore already making midterm victory their top priority, even though the elections are twenty months away and their party is in disarray. But who cares about that?

Biden knows how things work and has already pushed through his $1.9 trillion rescue plan, for which not a single Republican Senator voted. He tries to argue it was done in a bipartisan way because the plan is popular with the general public, which it is. Whether it was bipartisan in the way we generally understand is another matter.

Biden is now touring the country, selling a massive $2.3 trillion American Jobs Plan to the nation—which also has no Republican support—and does not even have the full commitment of all Democrats, for that matter. But we will have to wait and see how things work out. You would think infrastructure would be a bipartisan no-brainer, but apparently it's not. Even so, Biden remains intent on getting bipartisan support.

However, with the Republicans looking to the midterms, they don't want to work too closely with the Democrats, Biden is a man on a mission, and the Republicans do not want him to succeed. They probably have the advantage at the moment as it is rare for the incumbent party to do well at halftime; but like it or not, Biden's rescue plan was popular with the public as is his American Jobs Plan, even if it is scaled back.

Let's Have an Election, then Another, and Another

What's with this constant election fever? It's utterly crazy. As soon as a president elected, attention immediately turns to the midterm elections. The new president may well be given a one-hundred-day period of relative peace. But after that, the knives come out, and the focus is on the midterms.

So we all charge off toward 2022, but once the midterms have come and gone, does anyone then press the election pause button? Absolutely not! The conclusion of the midterms simply serves as a starting gun to look toward the presidential election. Even more crazy!

Through the eyes of this Englishman, I see the US as being locked in a constant round of wildly expensive, stifling, time-consuming, biennial elections, often hampering any president from implementing the policies for which they were elected.

But how did we get to this position in the first place? Well, it goes back a long way, so a quick look back in time is called for.

In 1787, when the country's population was barely four million, state representatives met in Philadelphia for the Constitutional Convention with the intention of giving more authority to federal government because at that time, almost all power resided with the then thirteen states; and that needed to be addressed.

This was to be achieved by amending the Articles of Confederation, but what resulted was a completely new document which reviewed the entirety of the political system. Today, this document is better known as the Constitution!

Among the many considerations was how long a president should serve; and delegates debated this subject at length, proposing a whole range of periods. Some, including Alexander Hamilton, argued in favour of a lifelong term, believing it would result in better decision-making in the absence of having to worry about reelection.

Thomas Jefferson, who was actually in Paris during the Philadelphia meeting, did not agree. He was concerned a lifelong term would degenerate into an inheritance. Hugh Williamson shared that view, saying he wanted to avoid an "elective king," who would "spare no pains to keep himself in for life" and would then "lay a train for the succession of his children." Williamson argued for a seven-year term but was open to a longer period.

Despite what were doubtlessly their best efforts, the delegates were unable to resolve the question and, remembering that old political adage "when in doubt, form a committee," appointed an eleven-member "Committee on Postponed Matters."

Some three and a half months after discussions first began, the committee proposed the president would serve for four years and could be reelected, but no limit was set for a maximum number of terms.

It was George Washington and Thomas Jefferson who established the two-term precedent as each of them stepped back after their second term. But not all subsequent presidents followed suit, although none went on to win a third term.

Franklin Delano Roosevelt, however, was an exception, and he served twelve years as president from March 1933 to April 1945. He died only a few months into his fourth term.

The reason he even ran for a third term was because the impact of the Great Depression and World War II had brought the country to a critical stage; and many felt FDR provided continuity, thus giving him the opportunity to run again.

It was because FDR served so long that after his death, Congress decided future presidencies should be limited to two terms. This was achieved through the Twenty-Second Amendment, which was introduced in March 1947 and ratified in February 1951.

But I've been thinking...

Let's Change the Presidential Term of Office Again

The way things work at the moment is not optimal, to say the least, so I think it's time for another change! We can look at what Hamilton, Jefferson, and Williamson said for guidance, which will ensure retaining a two-term, eight-year maximum period in office but with a bit of a twist.

Hamilton supported a lifelong term because it favoured better decision-making with no concerns about reelection. Jefferson and Williamson did not support the lifelong element with Williamson advocating for a seven-year term.

However, before changing the world, a quick reminder of the way it works today for a two-term president:

First term—president gets elected and works like mad to implement agenda ahead of the upcoming midterms, which will probably cost seats in Congress.

Post midterms—begins working immediately on getting reelected in two years' time. Gets reelected. Yippee!

Second term—deals with staff turnover (a traditional fifth-year phenomenon). Works like mad with new staff ahead of the upcoming midterms, trying to get back to the original agenda.

Post midterms—becomes ineffective as is no longer relevant. Authority and influence decline by the day, so works on legacy.

This is no way to run a railroad!

OK, so what is my cunning plan?

It is to replace the current two four-year terms with an extended first term of five years and a reduced second term of three years.

A five-year first term would allow time for better planning and implementing of policies. It would allow more time for the public to judge the president's performance and maybe even encourage more bipartisan cooperation. We can always dream!

The extra year in the first term would allow the interim elections to be pushed back from two years to three. This is critical as it would delay the current two-year mad dash between elections, giving the president time to create a following wind into the remaining two years of the first term.

When a second term is won, it is for an uninterrupted three years, thus enabling continued focus on "getting the job done" without more elections to worry about.

If a second term is not won, then the new president starts with a five-year first term.

What favours this change is that overall, a president gets much more time. Not only is there an extra year in the first term, but there's an extra year before interim elections. And the second term runs for three years uninterrupted.

This translates into one less election in an eight-year term. Just imagine how much time and money would be saved. A much better way to run a railroad!

But I would add two more requirements. First, anyone standing for election would have to produce the last, say eight years, tax returns; and the lame-duck period of about ten weeks between the election result and inauguration of a new president should be reduced to, say, six or eight weeks. Oh, yes, I nearly forgot—a president can only serve one five-year term, so tough luck if he or she is not reelected for a second term. Job done!

Confirmed: Liz Cheney Is Out

Before starting, let's review what Slippery Mitch and Whacky McCarthy said about Trump back in January.

McConnell, after the second impeachment trial, said of the 6 January riots, "The mob was fed lies. They were provoked by the president and other powerful people, and they tried to use fear and violence to stop a specific proceeding of the first branch of the federal government which they did not like."

McCarthy, speaking in the House, said, "The president bears responsibility for Wednesday's attack on Congress by mob rioters. He should have immediately denounced the mob when he saw what was unfolding."

Paraphrasing Cheney, all she did was to put out a tweet, saying One-Term was a liar when he claimed the election was stolen. She said he was "poisoning our democratic system." Nothing too dramatic there. But Whacky and other Republicans had her in their crosshairs; and after a twenty-minute secret vote on Wednesday, 12 May, she was out.

Unlike the first vote to oust her, which failed, this time, she did not try to get colleagues to rally round her. However, finally getting rid of her may not turn out to be the best move the Republicans could make.

After she was voted out, she briefly spoke with reporters and no doubt put a chill up McCarthy's spine—not that he has one—when she said, "I will do everything I can to ensure that the former president never again gets anywhere near the Oval Office." Wow! You could almost hear McCarthy saying, "Ooooh shit!"

The following day, NBC's *Today* show broadcast an interview with Cheney in which she made clear she was not going away, confirming she would "absolutely" run for reelection in Wyoming.

Trump and friends want Cheney out of her seat and are looking at ways to achieve that, but when asked about it, she was clear. "You know, bring it on. As I said, if they think that they are going to come into Wyoming and make the argument that the people of Wyoming should vote for someone who is loyal to Donald Trump over somebody who is loyal to the Constitution, I welcome that debate."

When asked if she would run against Trump in a Republican primary for the presidency, Cheney declined to comment. She did not say yes, but neither did she say no. Interesting!

However, Democrats would do well to remember that Cheney is definitely "not at all pro-Biden." When asked if she agreed if she had been pushed out because she was a distraction from the party being able to focus on Biden's policies, she said, "I've been very clear that I think President Biden's policies are dangerous."

So no ambiguity there. And she added, "Every single day, I am fighting against those policies and will continue to do that. My view is, to be as effective as we can be to fight against those things, our party has to be based on truth." Enough said.

Guess What? Arizona Goes for Another Recount

Yes, it's really true. When this was first reported, I thought it was a joke, but it's not! Arizona's Republican state Senate decided in their wisdom that after counts, recounts, audits, and failed court cases, that it was time for another recount, specifically of the votes cast in Maricopa County where Biden won a narrow but critical victory.

The count is being done by a company called Cyber Ninjas, which was founded by a "stop the steal" nutter, so no impartiality there! The company has no known track record in vote-counting, and the way things are going, that lack of track record is apparent.

The count started on 23 April and was scheduled to end by 14 May. Well, it didn't; and it's likely to continue to the end of June, if not beyond. The count is being carried out in secret, and the counters have had to sign nondisclosure agreements, ensuring a complete lack of transparency.

The whole thing is utter madness. One example of which is that some election-denying genius came up with the idea that China had flown in forty thousand fake ballots, so they are now looking for bamboo threads in the ballot papers! WTF? They're also looking for dodgy watermarks in other faked ballots! Frankly, if this wasn't serious, it would be hilarious. Actually, it is hilarious. Bamboo? Seriously?

But sadly, what's happening in Arizona could well give licence to similar recounts in other states, which would serve to keep the lie going and, by extension, would not bode well for the midterm elections.

The possibility of more violence cannot be ruled out, especially in the event of the "wrong result." It looks very much like what's happening now is laying the ground for more trouble to come. This does not look good, but I hope I'm wrong.

The Vote for a 6 January Commission

Immediately following the 6 January attack on the Capitol, politicians from both parties agreed a commission should be appointed to investigate the events that led up to the riots. However, with the passage of time and the interference of Trump, Republican interest is on the wane.

On 19 May, the House voted 252 to 175 to progress with appointment of a commission. On the face of it, a good victory, but it masks an increasing divide between the parties as over 80 percent of House Republicans voted against the commission's appointment.

In the days leading up to the vote, a stream of Republicans sought to downplay the events of 6 January. The best comments decrying the seriousness of the riots came from a new congressman and gun dealer named Andrew Clyde from Georgia who said that those entering the Capitol were acting "in an orderly fashion," and best of all, he said, "If you didn't know that the TV footage was a video of January 6, you'd really think it was a normal tourist trip." Go for it, Captain America!

But one thing about our intrepid hero that you should know, is there are two photographs of him during the tourist trip—the first where he is helping barricade the gallery doors, and the second where he is with his back to the wall, mouth wide open, terrified, looking like he's about to fill his pants. Presumably, he didn't want to take tea with the tourists.

What a disgrace! What a scared-of-Trump Republican!

But before we get off track, it is here we must bring in Slippery Mitch. Yes, he who was once seemingly in favour of a commission. Over a few short days, he gradually moved his position to the point that he was finally able to register his opposition.

He may be an arse, which he is, but he is also the complete politician. So screw what the right thing to do is. Forget about all those Capitol police officers who suffered serious injuries. Forget those who took their own lives. Forget that many of them are still recuperating. Forget why this whole shit-show happened in the first place. Forget everything—*I want to be head of the Senate!*

So next is the Senate vote, where, of course, it fails. The voting in favour of a commission was fifty-four to thirty-five—again a numerical victory for the Democrats but again falling short of the sixty votes needed.

However, the vote count showed that eleven senators did not even turn up to vote—nine Republicans and two Democrats. That is preposterous and is a complete abrogation of responsibility on their part. Shame on them.

What makes it worse is that McConnell, who was concerned that some Republicans would vote with the Democrats, was even more slippery than ever as he worked the phones the day before, asking senators to do him a "personal favour" and vote against the proposal.

This result is actually more disgraceful than it even appears, not because 306 members of Congress voted for a commission and only 210 against, but it disregards the will of most Americans. It disrespects all the officers who fought to defend the Capitol, and it totally disrespects the families of all the officers who died. Worst of all, it is exactly what Trump wants.

More practically, a commission would have thrown light on exactly how those events were allowed to happen and, crucially, given advice on how to avoid the same happening again. I fear this result leaves the door open for the same or something similar in the future. And for what? So Republicans improve their chances at the midterm elections. It's shameful.

Greene and Gaetz on Trump-Loving Tour

It was only a matter of time before these two wasters got together. They have launched a series of America First rallies, extolling the virtues of His Orangeness.

Greene, on stage in Florida, says to the crowd, "I just got to check something. I just want to make sure I'm in the right place. Tell me, who is your president?" The crowd shouts back, "Donald Trump!" Greene, happy at being able to motivate a bunch of morons, beams, "That's my president too." Pathetic!

At another rally, Gaetz says, "This is Donald Trump's party, and I'm a Donald Trump Republican!" Sadly, he's right about it being Trump's party.

He also made alarming remarks that, frankly, appeared to be inciting violence, saying, "The Second Amendment is not about hunting. It's not about recreation or sports. The Second Amendment is about the ability to maintain an armed rebellion against the government if that becomes necessary." This is not good!

We know that Greene can be just as incendiary and has regularly made trouble for herself. She was recently admonished—after a five-day delay—by House leader Kevin McCarthy for remarks made comparing the wearing of masks with the horrors of the Holocaust, comparing the Democratic Party to the Nazis.

Both Greene and Gaetz present a real problem for the Republicans. Nobody likes them, nor does anybody want to be associated with them. But they are 100 percent for Trump. And despite being disliked in Washington, DC, the crowds love them, and they have become almost untouchable.

But this is a problem of the Republicans' own making. Trump loves what these two loonies are doing, albeit from a distance, and the leadership did not tackle Greene and Gaetz early on when they had the chance.

They are now becoming more emboldened, and unless the Republicans take action against them soon, I can only see things getting worse and ending badly.

Trump Possibly in More Legal Jeopardy

Trump is already facing a raft of legal problems, but the list has recently been added to as a result of a new criminal investigation by New York attorney general Letitia James's office into the personal taxes of Allen Weisselberg and his role as longtime chief financial officer of The Trump Organization, although Weisselberg does not face any charges.

James's office says the investigation began partly as a result of documents provided by Weisselberg's former daughter-in-law, Jennifer Weisselberg, who has been in discussion with prosecutors since September 2020.

Also under investigation are Weisselberg's personal finances and benefits his son, Barry, received, an employee of The Trump Organization; and it is hoped with all this pressure, Weisselberg will be persuaded to cooperate with prosecutors.

Further investigations are purportedly looking at whether The Trump Organization gave financial benefits to its employees to compensate for lower salaries and into rent payments on Weisselberg's Manhattan apartment, according to a report by CNN.

Weisselberg has been with The Trump Organization for forty years and is known to have discussed all financial matters with Trump—father and son—and will know of all and any financial acrobatics, so if Weisselberg cooperates with James's team, this could turn out to be bad news for Trump and his family.

And taking a final look at Trump, it is common that history is kind to former presidents, but I cannot see One-Term enjoying such a courtesy. Forget about his personal flaws, just look at some of the people he associates with: Roger Stone, Rudy Giuliani, Steve Bannon, Paul Manafort, Michael Flynn—what a bunch of wasters. Look also at his two adult sons, his daughter, his son-in-law. None of these people give me the remotest sense of warmth. To a man, to a woman, they are self-serving.

Time to Wind Up

Knowing when to stop writing a book like this is never easy as there will always be loose ends. When I started, I had no idea when I would finish. At first, I wrote simply to keep busy during lockdown, but having started, I was encouraged by friends and family to continue. When I realised this was becoming a book, I would need to decide when to finish.

But for a story like this, how do you decide when enough is enough? I thought a logical end point would be at the conclusion of the presidential election in November. Well, that didn't work!

I then thought I would aim for Biden's inauguration, but that certainly didn't work as 6 January saw the Capitol Building coming under siege. The only other time the Capitol was stormed was in 1812 when invading British troops marched into Washington and set fire to it!

After Biden was sworn in, there was then the vote to impeach Trump for a second time—so another historical moment, which turned out to be when Liz Cheney and others fell seriously out of favour with their party for holding Trump responsible. Then there were vaccines, then the Derek Chauvin trial, then in May, Cheney is finally given her marching orders. When will this end?

I would not be surprised to see the midterm elections in 2022 become another defining moment in America's history. Trump, sadly, is not going away; and has even said he expects to be reinstated as president by August. He really is a screwball!

And talking of screwballs, I have to mention Ohio's super-crazy Dr. Sherri Tenpenny, who was invited recently to speak during a hearing of Ohio state legislators on the vaccine. And what did she say? She said vaccines make people "magnetized." WTF? She said people "can put a key on their forehead. It sticks. They can put spoons and forks all over them, and they can stick." It is so hard to believe that people like this really exist. But that's her story, and she's "sticking" to it!

Anyway, loose ends and all, I am closing now; and it's good to do so, seeing unemployment down from a frighteningly high 33.5

million in April last year to 9.3 million today and getting better. And coronavirus cases are declining from the heady three hundred thousand a day in early January toward ten thousand a day today with daily deaths also on the decline from the peak of nearly 4,500 in mid-January to around 300. Still lots to do, but it's good to finally have the feeling we are moving forward again. Please, no more surges!

There are so many memorable events that have taken place over the last nearly eighteen months, and I am glad to have documented some them as seen by me, an Englishman living in New York. At times, it's been funny. Often it's been sad, but it's always been rewarding! I just wish more people had been vaccinated.

In Closing, I Mourn the Loss of a True Friend

On 14 December 2020, I learned that one of my closest friends, Orlin Todorov, aged fifty-eight, had succumbed to coronavirus the day before. I cannot begin to express my sadness. Orlin and I were colleagues when I worked for an international bank in Bulgaria. During my seven years there, he was someone I relied on and whose counsel I always sought. We had quickly become friends and remained so for twenty-five years.

In 2003, two years after I left Bulgaria, Orlin left the bank to become chief financial officer of the country's largest oil distributor and then, a little over a year later, chief executive officer of its parent company, where he stayed until 2014.

In 2012, he and a friend, Dancho, had built twin properties on the Greek island of Rhodes. Adjacent to them was another piece of land on which they had the crazy idea of building four holiday villas.

In July 2016, I visited Orlin, his wife Biliana, and their young son, Bobby, then aged nine, in Rhodes; and we had a great time together. That was before Orlin and Dancho had planning permission or had arranged any finance for their new project, and I must admit I was skeptical that they would be successful.

By the end of 2017, after more than a year of struggles, Orlin wrote to tell me he had "yet another problem with the building licence." But typically, he never gave up; and in the end, he succeeded.

Only two months before he died, after four years of dealing with builders, bankers, and bureaucrats, Orlin sent me photographs of the completed project; and there they were—Serenity Villas! I was so impressed and proud of what he had achieved; and we agreed I would go there again the following year, coronavirus permitting.

From the moment I started recording my thoughts on this coronavirus mess, I never lost sight of the fact that the statistics we hear each day represent real people, and Orlin's passing is a cruel confirmation of that reality.

I would send Orlin updates of my writings, which he said he was always pleased to read. Ironically, I was just about to send him another update.

I find it hard to accept Orlin's passing, and I miss our conversations and exchange of messages. But as I mourn his loss, I am acutely aware that my life, and the lives of so many others, have been made so much richer thanks to his friendship; and for that I will forever be grateful.

From an earlier marriage to Chrissie, Orlin had two adult children, Andrey, or Andy as Orlin called him, thirty-four, and Kalina, who turned twenty-eight shortly after her father's passing. He was so proud of all his children, and rightly so.

Rest in peace, Orlin.

About the Author

Peter Rolls is a new name on the scene. He grew up in France, Singapore, Kenya, and England and was a keen sportsman, especially enjoying rugby and cricket. At one stage, he even considered pursuing a career in cricket but instead became a banker!

In his banking career, he continued his travels outside the UK, spending more than twenty years working in Europe, Eastern Europe, and Central Asia.

Today he is living and loving life in New York with his wife, and being an interested observer of the peculiarities of American politics and having always enjoyed writing, he has combined the two interests and finished his first book.

Lightning Source UK Ltd.
Milton Keynes UK
UKHW010707070223
416609UK00001B/267